Murder to Excellence: Growth & Development for the Millennial Generation

The Autobiography of
Wallace 'Gator' Bradley, Urban Translator

Wallace 'Gator' Bradley

& SaFiya D. Hoskins, Ph.D.

Foreword by Cornel West, Ph.D.

Copyright © 2014 Wallace Bradley and SaFiya D. Hoskins

Published by: Ubiquitous Press

All rights reserved.

ISBN: 0615886256
ISBN-13: 978-06158886251

For my beloved

Brothers & Sisters of the Struggle

CONTENTS

	Dedication	vii
1	Foreword by Dr. Cornel West	1
2	A Reflection by Jerry 'Iceman' Butler	5
3	Having a Moment	7
4	Path to the Penitentiary	20
5	Larry Hoover	40
6	Growth and Development	55
7	21st Century Vote	66
8	Consensus Candidate	75
9	Power Plays	82
10	Bogey Man	96
11	Urban Translator	106
12	Obama and West	118
13	Highest Regard	127
14	Ms. Ida and Terri	140
15	Pragmatism	147
16	Civics	153
17	Images	161

18	18-30 Theory	170
19	King David	175
20	Tributes	181
21	From 'The Blueprint'	246
	Acknowledgements	265
	Afterword	267
	Onward: To Stateville	272
	Photographs	276

DEDICATION

First and foremost, I would to dedicate this book to the women who have played a very important role in my life. There are a lot of women who have been in my life and the omission of their names here should not be perceived as a dismissal. I want to dedicate this book to my mother, **Ida Mae Rooks**, people called her **Ms. Ida**, when she married my father she became **Ida Bradley**. My only daughter, **Afrika LaShun Bradley**, and to my granddaughter, **Alexandria Amor Dillon** nicknamed **Alex**. To my sisters, **Donna Bradley, Patricia Bradley, Loretta Bradley** and **Aurelia 'Rico' Bradley**.

Also to **Congresswoman Maxine Waters, Reverend Willie T. Barrow, Mellody Hobson** and **Hermene Hartman**.

There are a lot of men who have played a significant part in the stability of my Growth and Development. Please know that I am not dismissing anyone who has not been named here. I want to dedicate this book to my father, **Wallace Bradley, Sr., Cook County Commissioner Jerry 'Iceman' Butler, Reverend Jesse Jackson, Prince Asiel Ben Israel, Judge R. Eugene Pincham, Appellate**

Growth and Development for the Millennial Generation

Court Justice Jesse Reyes, Appellate Court Justice Michael Hyman and **Appellate Court Justice Nathaniel Roosevelt Howse**.

Last and surely not least, I would like to dedicate this book to the **Honorable Larry Hoover, Sr.**

I would like to give a very special dedication to my sons, **Watari Marsh, Kahdmiel Malik Bradley, Leviticus Isaiah Bradley, Thomas Watson** and the **Honorable Noble Ameer Ali**.

I want to give a special shout-out to my brothers **James Kelly Rooks** and **Richard Bradley** known as **Frank Nitty**. My first cousins **Jimmy and Jerry Rooks**. Also to **Dr. Marvin Bradley, Kelvin Bradley** and **Preston Bradley**.

Shout-out to **Reverend Al Sharpton, William Beavers, Stan Rakestraw, John Rogers, Tim Rand, Cliff Kelley, Sherrie Sullivan, Attorney Elliot Zinger, Kahari Nash, Gerald Reed** and **J Prince**. A very special dedication to a close friend of mine **John Davis**; and, an honorable mention to **Jay-Z** and **Kanye West**.

The Autobiography of Wallace Gator Bradley, Urban Translator

1 FOREWORD BY DR. CORNEL WEST

Wallace 'Gator' Bradley is a living legend. He also is my dear brother whose courage and compassion inspire all of us to grow, develop and become better persons. Brother Gator has lived a rich and blessed life that starts on the streets of the south side of Chicago through the prisons of Illinois to the White House of the USA and back to the schoolrooms and playgrounds to serve young people. Like his favorite piece of biblical scripture – Psalm 140 – God has preserved him from violence, delivered him from wickedness and empowered him to fight for "the cause of the afflicted and the right of the poor."

I first met Brother Gator in the context of the gang summits that tried to bring peace and promote justice for our precious young brothers who have been socially neglected, economically abandoned and targeted by police surveillance. I was struck by Brother Gator's acute intelligence, genuine sincerity and soulful smile. It was clear he was my kind of brother – a brother shaped by the inimitable music of Curtis Mayfield, the spiritual struggle of Malcolm X and the visionary leadership of Larry Hoover. Fortitude and forgiveness, bravery and maturation, courage and conversion are shot through the life and times of Brother Gator. His powerful and poignant book is a testament to his strength and determination to be a force for good in the face of overwhelming odds. It charts his fascinating trek from the Racine Courts housing project to the racist courts of law in Chicago to his monumental anti-racist political activism in the historic campaigns of Jerry Butler, Jesse Jackson and Barack Obama. As one of the few ever pardoned by an Illinois Governor, Brother Gator has been an exemplary citizen in his adult life – with his loving and high-achieving wife and children, the great respect of fellow citizens for him and the high demands for his wisdom and skill from local, national and global leaders. He is an old school freedom fighter and new school urban translator whose actions and words lead us through the complex dynamics of Chicago criminal life, political life, prison life and moral service to poor people. Like Elijah Muhammad and Malcolm X, Brother Gator is a grand figure in the black freedom struggle who used past prison experiences to deepen love of and service to black people. I thank my dear sister Dr. SaFiya D. Hoskins for helping preserve the prophetic witness of Brother Gator for present and future crusaders for justice!

- Cornel West

Growth and Development for the Millennial Generation

Dr. SaFiya D. Hoskins, Wallace Gator Bradley and Dr. Cornel West

Dr. SaFiya Hoskins, Gator and Dr. West in dialogue

2 A REFLECTION BY COMMISSIONER JERRY 'ICEMAN' BUTLER

It is a typical cold January morning in Chicago, wind chill between 30 and 40 degrees below zero.

I am standing on the corner bus stop asking people on their way to work at six o'clock in the morning to sign my petition for candidate at large to the Cook County Board of Commissioners. A few feet from me is a brother hunched down in his overcoat, hat slanted to the side looking just a little bit shady shouting to passersby and commuters, "Come meet the Iceman, Jerry Butler he is running for Cook County Commissioner." Some people stop to say hello and sign the petition. Most ignore him and me; others say nothing, shake their heads no and keep walking as if we aren't even there, talk about a cold shoulder!

As I wait to say thank you for those who signed the petition list I wondered why is he here? Sure, I am hip as is he to the "Quid pro Quo." "Something for something," but this man is broke betting on the come. I am thinking there probably won't be any Quo for this Quid. His name is Wallace Gator Bradley and this book is his story.

3 HAVING A MOMENT

> It goes without saying, then, that language is also a political instrument, means, and proof of power. It is the most vivid and crucial key to identity: It reveals the private identity, and connects one with, or divorces one from, the larger, public, or communal identity.
>
> James Baldwin
> *If Black English Isn't a Language, Then Tell Me What Is?*
> (1979)

"I'm from the murder capital where they murder for capital…" is how Kanye West begins his verse in the song *Murder to Excellence* with Jay-Z on their multi-platinum album, Watch the Throne. The essence of what both Kanye and Jay-Z are saying is this; black-on-black murder has to stop. Kanye considers whether black-on-black violence is an act of genocide and Jay-Z says look, "…we on the same team. Giving you respect, I expect the same thing." These two young men have achieved global success and they are sending a message to the African American community through this song to warn that we have to stop killing each other. Jay-Z said, "Power to the people, when you see me, see you." The same way we have certain freedoms today because of the sacrifices our ancestors made; well, Jay-Z and Kanye are showing that they are a reflection of the power and the potential in African American communities everywhere. You can be as successful as both of them but you have to change the way you are thinking, the way you are living. In the profound lyrics of this powerful song Jay-Z and Kanye West are taking us to task. They are asking us to take responsibility, to be responsible for ourselves and the way our actions impact our communities. Like Kanye said, "It's time for us to stop and redefine black power."

Jay-Z and Kanye West are entrepreneurs and international celebrities but when they stopped in Chicago for their *Watch the Throne Tour* they made it a point to come back to the community. Any other multi-millionaire might wave at the people from a distance but Jay-Z and Kanye walked on 79th and South Shore among the people to show young adults that they no longer have to kill one another; we're all on the same team. They were out there showing their love and appreciation. If you watch footage from the exclusive video *The Chi* [on VOYR.com] you'll see the tour that Kanye West took Jay-Z on off the beaten path on the Southside. At the end of that video I feel that the words Kanye speaks are a message to the millennial generation (Or what I like to call the H.A.M. Generation; I'll elaborate later.) when he says:

We have to re-think, re-inspire. Wash the brain, don't brainwash. And allow people to think for themselves… But present amazing options to the best of what you know the truth to be. I feel like people can find themselves sooner.

The profound and prophetic sentiments expressed in the song *Murder to Excellence* is important for the millennial generation the same way that the Growth and Development movement helped to redirect previous generations. In the song Kanye asked another question that he leaves his listeners to answer, "What's the life expectancy for black guys?" To delve deeply into the answer to his question would be another book but his next line is on target, "The system is working effectively, that's why?" Jay-Z describes himself and Kanye as the "new black elite," he talks about being present next to the president. It is no secret that Jay-Z was an important part of rallying the Hip-Hop community behind getting the president into office and we all saw his beautiful wife perform the her version of the Etta James timeless classic, *At Last*, during the Inaugural Ball for Barack and Michelle Obama's first dance as the President of the United States of America and the First Lady. Jay-Z, Kanye, Sean Combs, Russell Simmons, Kevin Liles and a lot of other members of the Hip-Hop community came together to show their support for Barack Obama.

Growth and Development and the 21st Century Vote- like the message behind *Murder to Excellence* and the voting power shown by the Hip Hop community in 2008- is the vision of Larry Hoover. Larry Hoover is a long time close friend of mine and he has placed that vision in my life. I'm raising my children behind that vision. In the 90s, I was preparing young adults for the 21st century by telling them, like Malcolm X, that the 'ballot is more important than the bullet.' Although, we didn't know it then we were changing our direction and strengthening our ranks to use our power to elect the first African American president of the United States.

Our vision of Growth and Development expanded to include the creation of United in Peace. We met with gang leaders from all around Chicago and organized them to come together to assist our vision of going from the destructive power of the bullet to the constructive power of the ballot. So, those young adults in the 90s have become responsible adults in the 21st century behind the vision that Larry and I put together called, 21st Century Vote. The manifestation of that vision for the 21st century is Barack Obama being the president, Michelle Obama being the first lady and their two beautiful African American children [Sasha and Malia] with their African American grandmother [Marian Robinson]; all of them being in the White House.

What has happened behind the momentum of the *Murder to Excellence* masterpiece and then the 21st Century Vote is a movement I like to call, H.A.M. The acronym H.A.M. is like going hard, but instead of it standing for Hard As a Muthafucka- as in the song on *Watch the Throne* by the same title, H.A.M. stands for Having A Moment. There are 18 year olds having their moment in history by making sure that they come out hard. These H.A.M. young adults registered to vote in order to make sure that President Barack Obama remained the President of the United States for another term.

The H.A.M. Generation is real and I know the movement works because I took my son to register him to vote during the 2012 election year. I'm not talking to you about anything that I don't practice in my own home, in my own family. I could see the bridge between our efforts in 20th century for young adults in 21st century all over his face and I could sense how he felt once he got that certification. We stood together and took a picture right there in front of the Board of Elections. I saw that my son felt that this was his moment. He was 'having a moment,' so-to-speak. If my son lives to become 65 years old- and I pray that he will- then he can say to the youngsters when he becomes that age, "What did you do young man when you were 18? When I was 18, I made sure I got my ass out there and I voted and I helped Barack Obama secure his presidency for a second term and in Illinois I helped an African American woman become the first Supreme Court Justice in Illinois and I helped Jesse Jackson Jr. maintain his seat as Congressman of the 2nd Congressional District, that's where I lived."

As I imagined my son talking in his old age I couldn't help but to reflect on the moment that I had in my life-actually more like moments, so many moments, because I have been blessed to live to grow as old as I am. I lived to have the Rosa Parks moment, the Dr. Martin Luther King, Jr. moment, the Malcolm X moment, the Harold Washington election moment and low and behold the moment of Barack Obama. So, now the moment in my life is watching my son tell his partners, "It's time for us to have our moment by going hard to the polls." Watching him in his generation which is the H.A.M. Generation not Generation X- you follow what I'm saying.

The H.A.M. Generation is going hard to the polls because they learned from the *Watch the Throne* CD and listened to Kanye and Jay-Z talking about how they are 'about to go hard.' They're talking about going hard to excel so that others have to recognize who they are. Their power and brilliance cannot be ignored, just like the H.A.M. Generation. In *Murder to Excellence*, Jay-Z and Kanye West are sending a message and making a contribution to saving a generation by letting them know, 'hey we can show you how to become millionaires and not sell dope.' They say we know because we have been in the song *Murder to Excellence*, we have walked the streets and lived the life that inspired the lyrics and it is time to make a positive change.

In *Murder to Excellence* Jay-Z says, "Domino domino…" the higher he goes they ain't seeing nothing but Will Smith and Oprah. He's like, let's go back and bring millions higher with us because we know how to do it now, 'hey dude don't kill him, y'all come together and we can show you how you can become whatever you want to be in order to excel.' You don't need to have someone to accredit your level of intelligence. To watch my son feel that sense of confidence and competence of manhood was an incredible moment for me. He was 18, preparing to graduate from Simeon High School and coming into manhood. I told him, "Here's your first responsibility- not paying rent- but being a registered voter. Wear a condom and be a registered voter."

Seriously though, I told my son now you can feel the power that you have in your hand to make enough noise for them to hear you even if they don't agree with you. You've got the power to choose someone to an office where you can stand and say, 'hey I voted for you and I'm responsible for doing the right thing.' You've got the power to elect the president. You've got the power to elect a congressman. You've got the power to elect an alderman. You've got the power to elect judges. So now if you become a person of influence within the African American Community you'll reign from a city where the most powerful man in the western hemisphere, in America, President Barack Obama is from- Chicago. Dr. SaFiya is from Chicago, Kanye West is from Chicago, Larry Hoover is from Chicago and of course you know I am from Chicago. It makes me feel very proud to see how proudly my son took his first responsibility as a young adult and registered to vote, there is power in his vote- and yours.

Taking responsibility as a member of the H.A.M. Generation my son can say, 'Hey look dude I know Larry Hoover, I know about his vision, I know about Growth and Development that's why my pants aren't sagging.' No disrespect to those whose pants are sagging. But he can say, 'I know what is inside that book, *The Blueprint: From Gangster Disciple to Growth & Development*, and I understand the vision of Growth and Development.' My son knows that Growth and Development teaches that if you have less than a 'C' average you're in violation because ignorance is a violation. Those are rules in Growth and Development. My son can tell anyone, 'I know it doesn't say you're supposed to sell dope in Growth and Development and it doesn't say that you're supposed to kill in Growth and Development.' So, to see him walk out of that Board of Elections at 69 W. Washington and walk over to the County Building and through to City Hall to let his mother- who is working for Alderman Carrie Austin in

City Hall- know, "Ma I'm registered to vote. I'm a responsible young adult…" That shit was magnificent to me. So, when I tell others, I'm telling them no less than what I do for my own son. I am speaking to you, telling you, caring about your well-being and your future as I do with my own son.

Murder to Excellence is revolutionary. It is a powerful message to the H.A.M. Generation and radio stations don't want to play it because it is too radical. The song reminds me of when James Brown came out with *Say it Loud, I'm Black and I'm Proud* and when Marvin Gaye released, *What's Going On?* Those were songs that made you stand up with pride and those were songs that made you think about the betterment of the community. Those songs were a call to action. *Murder to Excellence* has that same power. Just think about when Kanye says, "I feel the pain in my city wherever I go, 314 soldiers died in Iraq, 509 died in Chicago." In that verse he's talking about black-on-black murder, here it is we have more people that were murdered on the streets of Chicago in one month than there were people who died in the war in Iraq. Ok?! These are profound things.

In 2009, Kanye West held a free concert at the Chicago Theater for Chicago students who excelled in their academic performance, classroom attendance and behavior in school. He did this as a part of the Kanye West Foundation that was established by his mother, the late Dr. Donda West. He has long been a part of contributing to uplift in the community. In *Murder to Excellence* Kanye mentioned watching the news and learning that a student who he had just been with was killed after school. He knows about the pain of black-on-black violence; it hurts him as much as it hurts us. Kanye and Jay-Z are talking about bringing awareness to a people and empowering a generation.

I love the CD, *Watch the Throne* because it is speaking so many truths about life. *Murder to Excellence* is especially one of my favorites because Jay-Z and Kanye are saying in so many words that black power is about loving one another instead of killing each another. Remember, these are young guys who went from selling CDs out the trunk of their cars and only wanting to be millionaires who drank Cristal and could 'make it rain' when they stepped inside the strip club to becoming millionaires in an industry that has exploded to the highest heights globally. They are a part of world where there is few blacks allowed entry; among them Will Smith and Oprah Winfrey. Jay-Z and Kanye are saying, 'damn we can go back and teach millions of others how to come up this way so it will be more of us,' when they reach the plateau where they currently sit.

The power of that song *Murder to Excellence* is evident when children are singing. You sense the power when you observe a ten year old listening to fifty year old people talking about the song *Murder to Excellence* and they interject to say, 'Nana, what Mr. Gator is saying is correct because all of us are listening to this song,' and then starts singing the song. At that very moment the ten year old child's conversation is on the level of a fifty year old, when everyone in the conversation understands the purpose of the song. Congressman Bobby Rush, a former member of the Black Panther Party in Chicago, can understand the words from the song *Murder to Excellence*. In the song Jay-Z let it be known that he was born on December 4th which was the day that Fred Hampton was brutally murdered by the Chicago Police Department and the Federal Bureau of Investigation. With that lyric Jay-Z is making a connection from his evolution to the revolution and across generations. That's the power of the song, *Murder to Excellence*. It has destroyed the gap between young adults and the elders. That's what it means.

Growth and Development was to Generation X what *Murder to Excellence* is to the H.A.M. Generation aka a generation of empowered young adults who are Having A Moment; their moment. So, as Kanye West said, "... let's savor this moment, and take it to the floor, Black

Excellence, Truly Yours."

4 PATH TO THE PENITENTIARY

And as a single leaf turns not yellow but with
the silent knowledge of the whole tree,
So the wrong-doer cannot do wrong without
the hidden will of you all.
Like a procession you walk together
towards your god-self.
You are the way and the wayfarers.
And when one of you falls down he falls for those
behind him, a caution against the stumbling stone.
Ay, and he falls for those ahead of him,
who though faster and surer of foot,
yet removed not the stumbling stone.
Kahlil Gibran
The Prophet (1923)

It's a struggle for every young Black man. You know how it is, only God can judge us.

Tupac Shakur (1996)

Wallace was born February 7, 1952, the third of eleven children of Wallace, Sr. and Eddie Mae Bradley. He grew up in the Racine Courts housing project on Chicago's South Side in the Morgan Park community made famous by Lorraine Hansberry in her play, 'A Raisin in the Sun.' He earned the nickname "Gator" from close friends and family, after the cartoon character "Wally Gator," a name he preferred to Wallace. Gator attended John D. Shoop Elementary School (now John D. Shoop Academy of Math, Science, and Technology) and had early aspirations of becoming an attorney. Upon graduation from Shoop he enrolled at Morgan Park High School...

On April 4, 1968, Dr. Martin Luther King, Jr. was assassinated. I was attending Morgan Park High School [on the South Side at 111th and Vincennes] at the time. When the announcement of his murder was made over the loudspeakers there was a moment of shock and disbelief- actually the shock never really went away- and a minute of silence. Some students and faculty broke down and started crying but a lot of the students were angry. Some of them began shouting their rage vocally but even more were showing their anger violently. Classes were adjourned early but not soon enough. Almost like a flash of lightening rioting started all over the school. That's when Rusty West and I, enraged by the death of Dr. King, grabbed a white guy- who was known to resent black students on campus- and threw him over one of the railings in the school.

After the incident at Morgan Park I ended up being sent to the 'Audy Home,' which is like juvenile detention. [Formerly the Arthur Audy Home for Children, the Cook County Temporary Juvenile Detention Center on the west side of Chicago has been labeled one of the worst of its' kind in the United States.] It was there that I got involved in pretty much the gang culture because it was the way of life and the only way to thrive in that community; and that's where I was living. Now, the Audy Home was on the West Side so they had the Vice Lords and I'm from the South Side so all of us from the South Side you know were like, together. We stuck together to make sure that the guys from the West Side didn't jump on a guy from the Southside. Inside the Audy Home I learned how to shoot craps and play cards. I also learned how to gamble and the conversation was all on the drug game; you know, and I learned about drugs.

[Thirty-three million adolescents were under the jurisdiction of the juvenile court system in 2006. According to data collected in 2011, two of every five adolescents confined to a juvenile detention center are African American and one in five confined adolescents are Hispanic. Clearly there are staggering racial disparities in the juvenile justice process when calculating that white youth comprise three fifths of the total youth population; yet, only thirty-seven percent of the total number of adolescents confined to juvenile detention centers. According to a report by the Annie E. Casey Foundation (2011):

> Compared to white juveniles, African American youth are: more likely to be formally charged (and less likely to have their cases dismissed or diverted from court); far more likely to be detained pending trial... less likely to receive a probation sentence... more likely to be sent to a state correctional facility... nine times as likely to be sentenced to adult prisons as white youth... the ultimate impact of these serial disparities is an enormous cumulative disadvantage for youth of color.

Furthermore, there are few reports of juvenile detention centers rehabilitating "criminally troubled" adolescents; conversely, high rates of recidivism (relapse into criminal behavior) are routinely reported. It has been estimated that anywhere from fifty to seventy-five percent of the young people who spend time in juvenile detention centers will be incarcerated later in life.]

When I was released from the Audy Home, I couldn't go back to Morgan Park because they had kicked me out. I also couldn't go to Fenger High School- the next closest school- because it was predominately white and they didn't want someone like me at their school who they feared might incite a riot on campus. Fenger was aware of my discipline record at Morgan Park- which had both black and white students- and they knew I got kicked out of Morgan Park because I was a radical. You know back then we were wearing dashikis because that was the way of life. I mean, "Say it loud I'm black and I'm proud," was real; you felt that. Everybody knew that a white guy had killed Dr. Martin Luther King, Jr.; we knew about Rosa Parks and women like her who were disrespected by white men every single day. We were motivated by Malcolm X and men like him to be proud and independent. That was the culture and culture was very strong then. So, they didn't want a guy who got kicked out of Morgan Park going to Fenger. I remember when we had to fight to go to Roseland (a once wealthy and predominately white south side community near Fenger; now poverty-stricken, rife with crime and inhabited primarily by African Americans and Hispanics). Can you imagine? We had to fight and protest just to go to the show! We had to cross that line! Fenger probably thought, 'Yeah we don't want this nigga in here startin' this shit. You know, we'll send him over there to Calumet with the rest of them.' [Regarding the school-to-prison pipeline the American Civil Liberties

Union (ACLU) stated in 2008, "There is no evidence that students of color misbehave to a greater degree than white students. They are, however, punished more severely, often for behaviors that are less serious."] So, that's how I ended up going to Calumet High School [now the Calumet Career Academy on 81st and May].

I wasn't at Calumet a minute before I got involved in the criminal activities taking place within the community, that's what I had learned at the Audy Home. I would burglarize, commit armed robberies and eventually got into selling drugs, the whole ten yards. Then I got arrested. I got arrested for burglarizing an auto business where they were selling tires, Vogue tires, for one hundred and fifty dollars each- that was a lot of money back then. When I caught my case for the burglary, Abe Thompson, the student body president, held a special assembly at Calumet to raise enough funds for my bail. The assembly was successful and they came and got me out of jail. I ended up getting probation for the burglary.

I was grateful for what the students at Calumet had done to get me out but I was committed to my emerging career as a criminal. Soon thereafter, I caught an armed robbery case for sticking up an after-hours joint. It was a high roller place; everybody in there had guns and drugs. I got caught because a guy walking past the joint saw me going in wearing a gray cashmere coat, a gray silk scarf and holding a pistol in my hand. He flagged down the police and the police came into the club; they found players in there with as many as thirteen guns. So, when I went to court none of the victims came and not one witness showed up. The judge said, "Well Gator, Mr. Bradley, we know that none of the witnesses or victims are coming to court for this armed robbery but you violated my probation. I can give you five to fifteen for violating this probation for burglary or I can give you four years and a day if you plead guilty to the armed robbery. I'll give you four years and a day for violating my probation and run it concurrent." So, I pleaded guilty to the robbery and took the four years and a day instead of letting him be able to give me five to fifteen. The math was easy.

The difference between then and now is when 'the powers that be' seize the young brothers and sisters caught up in the world of crime they are giving them time that takes them away for pretty much the rest of their precious young lives. Okay, when I was committing crimes I knew the time that I would get for the crime that I was committing. Today they can give an individual life in prison for being a part of a drug conspiracy.

When I went into the penitentiary everybody knew you by virtue of the fact of what community you came from.

Anyone inside was able to call back to that community and find out who you were and who you were connected with. So, for example, on the inside they knew Joe Schmoe by calling back to his community. They knew that, 'Hey if you rape him, five of y'all may rape him; but, y'all are going to get killed because he ain't going to stand to see you live.' So, basically if you take his ass you can get ready to have something stuck in your neck. They say, 'don't fuck with him because he's crazy or he's a fool.' They knew by your associations from the street or what you did on the outside. The little guys who are committing crimes today will shoot someone down in a heartbeat, they're talking real tough. Can't 'nobody' touch them out in the streets but when they get behind them walls they break down like little girls- for lack of a better phrase. No disrespect to girls, because girls got into the penitentiary the same way; they're catching hell too just like those niggas are catching hell.

When I went into the penitentiary we pretty much had control over the institution; all that's changed now. The guys in there today have a little control over it but not like they used to have. When they go in now, these guys are on the street saying or they're on the street talking about, "We doin' it in Larry Hoover's name. We doin' this in GDs name." I ask them, "Well are you are a Gangster Disciple or for Growth and Development?" If they respond, "Well, I'm a GD." I have to tell them, "Nah, if you're a Gangster Disciple that doesn't even exist anymore more. Larry Hoover's name is not even attached to that anymore; these are the rules." So, when they talk that shit and when they get in the penitentiary and they don't know what's really going on, they get dealt with.

These tough talkers shout about how can't nobody tell them what to do out here on the street; but, all of a sudden when they get behind them walls the first thing that 'the man' tells them to do is you have to bend over and spread your cheeks to make sure there isn't any contraband. When you go in there- all of us- you have to strip naked. I don't know anybody, I don't care if it was Jeff Fort, Larry Hoover, me or anybody that knocked that individual over who told us to strip naked, you follow what I'm saying. So, you learn that when they tell you to get up at five o'clock in the morning and stand in front of that cell, you better stand up in front of that cell. You can't shout that you say out here, 'Can't nobody tell me when to get up and out and all that.' All that shit is changing.

Rehabilitation was the order of the day when I went into the penitentiary. Right now rehabilitation is not the order of the day. 'The system' wants young adults to keep going back in and out of the penitentiary because it's a corporation now and if I've invested in the penitentiary then making sure that you go back in and out and in again to that penitentiary is helping me with my investment; this is how the 'prison industrial complex' operates. The penitentiary is now on the stock market, okay. ["But prisons do not disappear problems, they disappear human beings. And the practice of disappearing vast numbers of people from poor, immigrant, and racially marginalized communities has literally become big business." Angela Davis, *Masked Racism: Reflections on the Prison Industrial Complex*, 1998.]

So, when I went in I already knew the deal. I made the decision what time I wanted to get for the crimes I had committed; the judge let me know that he had the power and then he gave it to me. So, I'm sitting there; instead of getting five to fifteen I had four years and a day. My mind was focused on rehabilitation. I thought, 'I'm not trying to get caught back up in this shit no more.' I made a decision to change for better.

Inside the penitentiary there were rules that I would have to follow along the road to rehabilitation. I made it my business to learn and follow those rules. Here are the rules- and they're pretty simple- if you're behind the wall then you are dealing with 'tickets'- a ticket is like when they tell you to do something and you don't do it and they send you to the hole and that type of shit; ok, that's a ticket- that can take away from your time or give you more time. I know I got one ticket when they brought my daughter, Africa, down to see me. The visiting tables had a little glass thing to separate the prisoners from their guests. We were seated at one of those tables with the little glass thing between us; I reached over it to the other side and grabbed my daughter. The guards told me I couldn't do that; I said, 'okay' and they put me down in the hole. I was pretty new there at the time but they felt like, 'You just got in here but we're going to show you that you have to obey the rules.' That's the only one ticket I earned but it was pretty much understandable. You know, well shit, a nigga trying to hold his kid because it ain't no telling if he'll be able to see his kid when he get back out because the mother could hook up with somebody else, take your child away from you and all that type of shit- it's understandable. Thankfully, Africa's mother never did anything to sever my relationship with my daughter. So, the rule book says that if you don't get a ticket within a year then you get to go to what they call the 'honor bar.'

The honor bar was a place in the penitentiary where there were guards but there were no bars, you follow what I'm saying. You'd either have your own room or you'd sleep in a dormitory. You could go out when your visitors came; you all could have picnics; you could have sex on the yard; and, all kind of shit. I ended up on the honor bar for not getting a ticket within a year. Once on the honor bar if you don't get a ticket within one year you end up going to the work release center which is back on the street. I didn't get a ticket while I was on the honor bar and I ended up being sent to the work release center. Now, all this time it's like I'm detoxing from the criminal psychological energy that was in me in order to make myself become a society driven person- you know- to be able to be back out in society, to be respected, to be free.

It was my responsibility to make sure that I had a job waiting for me before I arrived to the work release center. By virtue of having employment, I would be able to roam the street and be free and come in and check in and take my key and go in and get out and catch the bus and go to the movies, you know all those things. My father was doing construction- you know I'm a junior, his name was Wallace- and the mob was pretty much in control of the union. My father was working for the Caruso family as a general labor foreman. Jesse Jackson and others had once come to the site with intentions of having it shut down on the accusation that there were no blacks being employed there. Well, my father was the first black general labor foreman for the Caruso family. He came out with some more workers to show Jesse and the others that there were indeed black individuals employed at the site. My father said, "Hey now y'all can get on up off this site 'cause we're working here." Besides, everybody knew back then that Jesse was shaking people down too, you know what I'm saying. To show his appreciation for what my father had done Caruso made sure I had a job in the construction industry when I came out the joint. So, I came out now and I've got a job. I pretty much didn't have to hump in the street or none of that because I was doing construction. So, that's how I came out the penitentiary.

Today, when offenders are sent to the joint there aren't any rehabilitation programs available. The schools have been taken out of the penitentiary. Ex-cons were coming out of there- back in the day- with PhDs and everything else. They were making themselves become and qualifying themselves to be constructive citizens within society. So, now all of these programs are out of the penitentiaries. [According to a UCLA School of Public Policy and Social Research study, 'Correctional Education as a Crime Control Program,' (2004):

One million dollars spent on correctional education prevents about 600 crimes, while that same money invested in incarceration prevents 350 crimes. Correctional education is almost twice as cost-effective as a crime control policy.]

As a rule in prison they say, 'Well you can't smoke in here.' No smoking is fine, it's a healthy thing I don't see why anybody should have to smoke; but, then smoking might calm nerves or make the time easier for some individuals- maybe even keep them from snapping on someone. So, they enforce 'no smoking' but they don't have any programs that help prisoners become productive citizens. When these ex-cons hit the street they tell them because you were in the penitentiary you are not allowed to stay in this part of public housing- you follow what I'm saying- and if your wife is staying in public housing with your children you can't even go and stay there because you're an ex-felon. In essence, they are making it where ex-felons have nowhere to go but back to the world of crime and eventually back to prison- you know what I mean- it's by design.

Even with a budget proposed by President Barack Obama you can see where he has cut all kinds of programs that have been helping poor people and African Americans. You almost can't help but to be like, 'Damn what's really going on?' As Obama was delivering his 2012 State of the Union Address he never even mentioned poor people; if you look at the whole speech the word poor is nowhere to be found. Despite this fact, when he put the budget out you see the first programs he has to cut are for the poor people. It's like Malcolm X said in his April 4, 1964 speech, 'The Ballot or the Bullet':

> ...They get the entire Negro vote, and after they get it, the Negro gets nothing in return. All they did when they got to Washington was give a few big Negroes big jobs. Those big Negroes didn't need big jobs, they already had jobs. That's camouflage, that's trickery, that's treachery, window-dressing. I'm not trying to knock out the Democrats for the Republicans. We'll get to them in a minute. But it is true; you put the Democrats first and the Democrats put you last.

Despite having been put on the 'pay no mind list,' it is not in our DNA as a people to perish. It has been Hell for niggas in America, it's going to always be Hell for niggas in America- but we always get through it. There are individuals out there thinking about me, 'Even though all the shit he went through...' they still hate Gator and they still talk shit about Gator. 'He been out the joint 30 years, got a pardon, and went to the White House...' and they still talk about me as if I'm out there leading a world of crime. They are actually out there and they hate me for doing right! So, this book is showing them and my life is proving to them that you can do what you want and man fuck it. I don't care what you say about me; but, don't tell me I don't have a right to earn a honest living for my family. The absence of rehabilitation programs in prisons is only assisting poverty and disabling ex-offenders from effectively taking care of themselves and their families. [In his 2008 article, *Incarceration vs. Education Reproducing Racism and Poverty in America*, Dr. Manning Marable asked:

> What are the practical political consequences of the mass incarceration of black Americans? In New York State, for example, the prison populations play a significant role in how some state legislative districts are drawn up. In New York's 45th senatorial district, located in the extreme northern corner of upstate New York, there are 13 state prisons, with 14,000 prisoners, all of whom are counted as residents. Prisoners in New York are disenfranchised—they cannot vote—yet their numbers help to create a Republican state senatorial district. These "prison districts" now exist all over the United States.]

In that penitentiary it 'ain't no joke,' like Rakim said in his 80s rhyme. When offenders go in there now and they don't know anyone they are in deep trouble. Just like O.J. Simpson, okay, he didn't want to be around black folks, you know, he loved the white folks and everything else; he ended up in the joint because he was messing around with white folks. A nigga would have never told him, 'Man let's go in there and take a trophy,' you follow what I'm saying. The white folks told O.J. that bullshit and set him up. He ended up in the joint; brother got beat so bad and he probably got raped too, you follow what I'm saying. O.J. standing 6'2" and over two hundred something odd pounds was in the infirmary for 3 weeks; so clearly, the penitentiary is no boys and girls club. Young people need to know that there is no glorification in going to prison. Ain't no grandeur; no how, no way, shiiit. It's a mother's worst nightmare.

I was a criminal that knew how much time that I was going to get for the crime that I committed. The fact that I knew the time for the crime made me like a career criminal type of guy; you know that was my career. So, it's like if I took a career to be a plumber I knew how much money I would make to be the plumber, you follow what I'm saying. These days a career criminal who doesn't know how much time that he's going to get for the crime that he commits; well, he's just a dumb crook. So, that's the difference.

The young adults committing crimes now don't even take in account how much time that they can get for the crime that they commit. And what I mean by that is, let us say the law was that you stand the chance of getting probation with one hundred grams of powder cocaine but if you get caught with six grams of rock cocaine you get six to thirty years. [Evidence of "an unjust criminal system with differential treatment of majority versus minority drug habits- white middle-class cocaine versus ghetto crack" (Cornel West, Hope on a Tightrope: Words and Wisdom, 2008).] So a criminal wouldn't say, oh well give me the six grams- and I'm not justifying crime I'm just telling you how it goes- a criminal would say, well give me one hundred grams of powder cocaine. A crook, 'give me uh, man give me ten grams of rock 'cause I can get uh mo' money.' He hasn't even thought that you can get probation or you can get six to thirty. Then when he gets caught he says, 'maaan, man that's bogus man they gave me...' Dude! It was written in black and white. One hundred grams of powder cocaine can get you probation; ten grams of rock gave you six to thirty. You follow what I'm saying? It's like that, and the majority of the people who are locked up in the penitentiary is because of rock cocaine, crack. Am I right or wrong?

When you look at the situation it isn't the white folks- you can't blame them- it's us. Now don't get me wrong, they targeted us by systematically discouraging our relationship with books and knowledge through mis-education and social and psychological warfare [Read 'Mis-Education of the Negro,' by Carter G. Woodson]; but, just as many people have fought to learn and died for our right to read. We should know better as much as they know how to catch us up, and there's a saying, "If you don't want a black person to know anything just put it between two covers like it's a book." Chris Rock joked, "What you have to do is if you really want hide your money put it between the cover of a book. They ain't going there." But seriously, the laws are all right there between two covers. The laws can even be Googled and found right there on the Internet. You can't expect them to spoon-feed this information to us; they are counting on your ignorance. It is our responsibility to read the books, the table of contents, the footnotes, the index, the fine print and everything else. That's how you know the rules- the laws- and learn how to play the game. You have to read. If today you read then tomorrow you will lead.

5 LARRY HOOVER

Larry Hoover, one of the founders of the notorious Gangster Disciples has paid his debt to society and is now being held under federal jurisdiction on trumped up charges based on constitutionally inadmissible evidence, the poison fruit of entrapment.

Growth & Development, Hoover's new ideology has helped thousands of former gangbangers and other misdirected souls transform into responsible members of society. To deny Mr. Hoover's rehabilitation and other who continue to benefit from it, is to ignore the divinity & power of the hu-man spirit and will to BE what it chooses.

Who else better qualified to show others the way, than one who was lost and has found the way? The sub-cultural, criminal dynamic that has evolved from the past, is the institutional cash-cow of today, huh? Man that's straight bullxxxx, and if we ain't careful, we all fall down!

Freelarryhoover.org (2011)

The Autobiography of Wallace Gator Bradley, Urban Translator

My friendship with Larry [Hoover] started I want to say around 1971. He knew a friend of mine, Rusty West. See Rusty West was the leader of the Lynchmen and I came up under Rusty. So, when Larry Hoover was branching out to connect all of the gangsters from around the city that's when I first met, Larry Hoover. We met in the Racine Courts [on the South Side at 107th and Racine Avenue] right there behind Ms. West's house [Rusty's mother]. You see, in 1971 the Lynchmen were hooking up with Larry Hoover and the Gangster Disciples to become the Lynchmen Sercon Gangsters. They were all joining together under the umbrella organization, Black Gangster Disciple Nation, and it's like we- for lack of a better phrase- we were all a band of criminals, so to speak. So, the things that Larry Hoover may have been doing in his community were also happening out in our community; it's just that Larry Hoover wanted to do those things in our community and we wanted access to Larry Hoover's community. It was like we were all lions coming together saying, "ain't no sense in us trying to make a play on another lion." You know what I mean? 'We are all over the lambs and we will share the lambs.'

Before long, we all ended up in Cook County Jail for various different crimes. For the crimes we committed in our community and the crimes that Larry Hoover committed in his community we all ended up in one community, which was at 26th and California. From there we all wound up in the Illinois Department of Corrections. [The Illinois Department of Corrections, IDOC, was established in 1970 and located in Springfield, Illinois.] Myself, I had two brothers locked up with me at the same time. The youngest named Tyrone Bradley was called Frank Nitty and another brother, named James Kelly. Eventually, the three of us were moved to the Stateville Correctional Institution [in Crest Hill, Illinois where in 1994 the serial killer John Wayne Gacy was executed by lethal injection.] Larry Hoover was there and a lot of the GDs, the Disciples, everybody was there. ["While incarcerated Larry Hoover helped form the Folks Nation which added other gangs such as: Black Disciples, Gangster Disciples, Imperial Gangsters, La Raza, Spanish Cobras, Latin Eagles, Maniac Latin Disciples, Simon City Royals, Spanish Gangster Disciples, Two Sixers, Young Latino Organization Disciples, Young Latino Organization Cobras, Black King Cobras, and International Posse... Hoover's power seemed only to grow inside Stateville. He began protecting other inmates, who then became devotees and new recruits for the Gangster Disciple Nation. His control over the other prisoners was recognized by the warden's office, which began looking to

Hoover as a positive influence to quell riots and uprisings within the prison system."- Wikipedia.]

Let me give you a quick history lesson, see when Larry Hoover hooked up with David Barksdale, original leader of the Black Disciples, there were three major gangs in Chicago. The city had the Stones, the Gangsters and there were the Disciples. We were a form of the Gangsters and so when we hooked up with Larry Hoover and then Hoover hooked up with Barksdale we became Black Gangster Disciples. Or part of the Black Gangster Disciple Nation [also known as BGDN.] Although we were part of the Gangster Disciple Nation we were still known as the Lynchmen Sercon Gangsters. While in the Stateville Correctional Institution we built up on that name and reputation.

I had pled guilty to armed robbery and burglary because I had probation for the burglary charge. When I caught the armed robbery charge none of the witnesses would come to court neither did any of the victims appear in court for the armed robbery trial. Since I already had probation for the burglary charge the judge told me he would just give me five to fifteen for violating his probation.

It was let me see, 1971 and I was born in 1952, I have to say I was nineteen or maybe twenty years old. The judge told me that he would give me four years and a day if I pled guilty to the armed robbery and he would give me four years and a day for the burglary. You know, run it concurrent. So, I said okay give me four years and a day- because I can count. If he would have given me five to fifteen I would have had to do five years first and then take my chances with coming out on parole. During that time they could tell you that you have to come back to the parole board in two years and the next time it will be nine years. So, I took four years and a day.

At that very moment in time, I changed my mind. I made the decision not to allow 'the system' to get me caught back up in 'the system.' I changed my whole persona. You know what I'm saying? No longer was I going to be a stick up man. No longer was I going to be a burglar coming through the ceiling of different businesses. I changed my whole thing around and I stopped cold turkey.

I planned to come out of the penitentiary. I saw that if you didn't make a mistake behind the wall like getting tickets- or whatever it is- you would go to the honor bar and when you get to the honor bar if you don't get any tickets you are sent to the work release center. When you are on your way to the work relief center that means they are putting you right on the street. When you got on the street if you had a job then you got furloughed. So, I worked my way through the system like that; that is what rehabilitation is all about- 'getting out of the system.'

Larry knew that out of all the guys in Stateville, I had a way out. Everybody else had been caught with crimes where they had anywhere from ten to fifteen years and twenty to life or life. You follow what I'm saying? Larry knew even then that I have what is known as, 'the gift of gab.'

I was released from Stateville, in 1975, into the work release program and I went to work doing construction. The construction company I worked for was being run by a real mob family, the Carusos (as I mentioned earlier). They were a part of the Italian Mob called the 26th Street Mob. The family patriarch, Frank T. Caruso, used to run with Sam "Momo" Giancana as the leader of the Forty-Two Gang and is related to former First Ward Alderman Fred Roti by marriage. The reason I am mentioning the Carusos is because almost two decades after I had worked for them- when few others would employ a newly released convict- I had the privilege of returning the favor.

In 1997, Frank Caruso's son Frank Caruso, Jr. was arrested along with several other youths from Bridgeport for beating Leonard Clark into a coma somewhere near Cellular Field. Well, it was his grandfather, Frank T.

Caruso, who had looked out for me. You see, Frank Sr.'s old man was in the construction business and the one who got me the job doing construction in the 70's. His son had jumped on this unsuspecting black guy for being over in Bridgeport- simply because Bridgeport was an area where they did not like to see black people, let alone catch black kids. Well, the entire African American community was getting ready to go over to Bridgeport and fight. Even all of the African American street organizations were banding together to go over there on the general principle of 'how are all these white guys going to jump on this one black kid?!'

To make a long story short, Frank Sr. told me, "Gator, I want to talk to you." He reasoned with me, "Don't go over in Bridgeport and have that picnic. The guys want to talk to you 'cause they don't want to have a race riot." So, I went over and talked to the guys. Now all the time I didn't know that this was the same family that helped me when I came out the joint and because they helped me get a job I didn't go back to the penitentiary. I was doing Frank a favor but I didn't know how deeply the family was involved. When I got over there to talk with the guys, Frank Caruso Sr. told me, "Gator, my son was wrong for being with them guys that jumped on that black guy. You know I've never had a problem with the black community.

Me and Harold Washington was cool and everything." He said, "I just want my son to get a fair trial and whatever happens after the trial so be it." So, what could I say? His old man helped me. His son was not born until years later; but, out of honor I chose to go out and demand his right to a fair trial.

I organized a group to protest outside the court for Frank Jr.'s right to a fair trial. Meanwhile, the black community was like, "Man Gator, how you going with them white kids?" My response was, "Look, just like when a black person hurts or kills someone's black kid you all would be coming to me and demanding that that kid have a fair trial. What the fuck is the difference? Everybody is entitled to a fair trial." You know they really took me through it. You know what I'm saying? The Caruso family admitted that it was wrong what their son did and Frank, Jr. was sentenced to eight years in prison. Larry Hoover and had sent word through the joint that nobody should put their hands on Frank Caruso, Jr. and you know it was all peace. The family took care of Leonard Clark, his mother and his family. Frank Sr. taught Clark how to ride a horse, helped him learn to drive and with his studies. The Clark family became friends with the Caruso family and would even go down to visit Frank Jr. in jail. So everyone who had been so opposed to Frank, Jr. during the trial was silenced like, 'umm.'

The Sun-Times later did a front page story on Leonard Clark and Frank Caruso, Jr. saying Leonard Clark was in Bridgeport stealing their bikes. So, okay he was not a good kid; so, he got caught doing wrong; so what? I saw Leonard Clark in 2012 and I didn't know who he was. He was working in the State of Illinois building. Leonard Clark went from being a ruffian in the streets to working for the state. He came a long way from allegedly stealing bikes in Bridgeport.

I'm saying that to say, when an individual gives you his word and you give him your word, your word is meant to be stood on- for lack of a better phrase. Standing on your word means that what you say is solid or trustworthy. Everything turns out right when you honor your word.

When Larry gave me his word on changing the organization's name and mission from Gangster Disciples to Growth and Development saying, "This is what we've got to do Gator. You're out and you know we're in." I took his word and I took him at his word and I stand on that vision of Growth and Development. When I went to the Oval Office and I met with Bill Clinton they knew I was there representing Growth and Development. They knew I was there representing Larry Hoover as well as the African American community. They knew that Larry

Hoover and I talked on the phone the day before I went to the Oval Office. I know they knew because in Larry Hoover's trial they brought up the picture with me in the Oval Office and played the taped conversation with Larry telling me to go and meet with the president so that everyone will know what's going on in the community.

My advice, be careful what you do today because you never know what is in store for you tomorrow. ["Follow the three R's: Respect for self, respect for others and responsibility for all your actions."- Dali Lama]

Larry Hoover began work on the charter for Growth and Development in the 80s. We were still in touch with each another although he was behind the walls. I was going back and forth down to the joint to visit my brothers, Nitty and James Kelly; and I used to go and visit Larry. The full manifestation of the Growth and Development piece did not really gel together until around I will say probably about 1985 and 1991. We he had about four or five chief enforcers. Larry had them working the streets. I will put it this way; I was one of his chief enforcers to help enforce the peace initiative. Around that same time is when Larry came into dealing with the United in Peace Movement.

I had always been a chief enforcer for Larry Hoover. However, being a part of Growth and Development I had become an enforcer for peace. I'll put it this way, just like the Secretary of State, Hilary Clinton, was for peace- and now John Kerry- but they know that she was a force to be reckoned with. Any individual who is going out of his or her way to create a violent atmosphere has repercussions coming. So, if you're fighting to stop peace, then I had to enforce the peace. I just was not the enforcer only going around on a mission shaking people down. There are all different kinds of enforcers, for all levels. I was not the enforcer going to tell individuals, 'Uh, hey I'm going to break your legs if you don't give me uh street tax,' or whatever that shit is. However, I would have that same intensity. If I came and said, "Hey man you ain't supposed to have that pistol at this event," an individual would have to comply or get dealt with. There are repercussions for individuals violating what was agreed to for all street organizations.

Growth and Development was a widely publicized initiative and everyone knew about my new rank as peace enforcer, all of this was publicized. The media covered the organization's shift widely because, at this time the former Mayor of Chicago, Eugene Sawyer, had gone to the parole board on Larry Hoover's behalf. There were large communities of people who supported his effort and the aims of Growth and Development.

In addition to working with Larry, I was working with the Cook County Chairman, Jerry Butler. I was his campaign manager and it had become a city-wide issue that Jerry Butler was going to hire this 'gangster' to work for Cook County with him because he had become the Chairman of the Law Enforcement Law Committee of Cook County. Within that committee you had the state's attorney office, the public defender's office, the sheriff's department, the county jail and all of these departments were under his purview. When the County Sheriff and his assistant met with me and Jerry Butler he was like, "Well Jerry you sure you want this guy Gator to be working with you?" Jerry told him, "I'd rather have him working with me 'cause I know he ain't trying to go back to the penitentiary." Ironically, the Deputy Sheriff for the sheriff who was supposed to be investigating me ended up going to the penitentiary for corruption.

Every other gang leader had gone in and out of the penitentiary like two hundred million times. I could never comprehend why they wanted to keep Larry Hoover in the joint when I saw him making so much progress and doing so much in the community. He was telling young brothers on the street not to kill one another. He was even enforcing the fact that they had to go to school. You know what I'm saying? There was no hanging out around the schools. There were no drugs being sold around the schools. If the school had BDs and GDs you started to see hall monitors that were BDs and GDs to make sure there were no gangs fighting in the schools and to make sure the halls were clear of anybody hanging around. Everybody had to be in their class. When he had effected change in the schools all the elected officials started saying, "man, Hoover if you could just get the young adults registered to vote." So, he put the order out to get young adults voting, just like that.

In the joint, Larry arranged things where it was mandatory for all of us who went into prison as functionally illiterate had to go to school. All of us, including Hoover had to learn how to read and everything; I got my GED in the penitentiary. You have brothers who have gotten college degrees. You have brothers who have taken paralegal classes, and that's why all of us understand law. You even have brothers who have gotten individuals off of death row and put back on the streets and everything else. So, out of all the organizations it was like we were more regimental and regarding education known to come out the penitentiary a better product than we were going in.

Larry Hoover had a vision and a plan for rehabilitation and reform in the penitentiary. We all came out with a better outlook. I don't know anybody else's structure but the Gangster Disciple structure was tight. It was so tight that once I had ended up in the Oval Office the U.S. Attorney said, "Hey we got to stop them." You follow me? You know and it was so deep; they were even trying to give me a car theft. Somebody stole a rental car and they knew that I didn't steal the rental car; the car was rented for me by a gentleman named John Davis. They knew that it was an element out there that didn't want me to be in the oval office meeting with a president. You follow what I'm saying? Okay, and so they got me a ride- it was a white Cadillac- so I could get around. Come to find out the security people at the airport for Avis were using the Cadillac that was rented to me in scams like the car was rented or it was stolen and all that type of shit, right. The young lady who rented me the car didn't know it was used. I didn't find out about all of this until I went to court. I ended up suing them for 120,000 dollars and I won the case.

Despite early concerns by some ranking government officials and despite some of their plans for intervention, I made it to the White House. I'm the only person who I know that was from a street organization who met with a sitting president in the Oval Office to talk about solutions to challenges plaguing the urban community. The same issues I took the White House were matters that had already been discussed with Larry Hoover. They were concerns being addressed by Growth and Development.

6 GROWTH & DEVELOPMENT

History shows, then, that as a result of these unusual forces in the education of the Negro he easily learns to follow the line of least resistance rather than battle against odds for what real history has shown to be the right course. A mind that remains in the present atmosphere never undergoes sufficient development to experience what is commonly known as thinking. No Negro thus submerged in the ghetto, then, will have a clear conception of the present status of the race or sufficient foresight to plan for the future; and he drifts so far toward compromise that he loses moral courage.

Carter G. Woodson

The Mis-Education of the Negro (1933)

Growth and Development for the Millennial Generation

I'm going to tell you about 'Growth and Development.' It's called going from Gangster Disciples which is the negative to Growth and Development which is the positive. *The Blueprint: Gangster Disciple to Growth and Development* [a book written by Larry Hoover with Rod Emery] is our manifesto and a of code ethics so-to-speak. They can try to declare it is all about gangs but it's not. 'Growth and Development' is a code that we live by which states that you should only aid and assist in righteous endeavors. For example, if you commit a crime against someone like sticking them up, that is not a righteous endeavor. Or another example, selling dope is not a righteous endeavor.

The Growth and Development manifesto states that you need to be about your 'Five Ps' or in other words, 'proper planning prevents poor performance.' So, you don't run out there in the streets- or the world for that matter- and just do something without first sitting back and thinking and planning and then working the plan. Our manifesto also teaches about wisdom; knowledge and understanding; and, love, life and lord. That is my platform- or my code of ethics- it was ordained and we received it from Brother Larry Hoover. For this reason, you can go to my webpage and read where it is explained that because of his vision I was able to see my way out the penitentiary, that's a powerful vision.

I apply the 'Growth and Development' manifesto to my everyday life even to the point of telling my children that 'Growth and Development' is a code to live by. I tell my sons, "If a random guy comes up to you, says he's a gang leader, and trying to get down with you, and then talks about your daddy once being a leader of the same gang, you just look at them and check their chorus book," which is a grade book in school [or report card]. My sons know if the supposed gang leader has a 'D' average you can't mess with them because in our literature as an individual it is mandatory that you get an education, it is required. I tell them, "If somebody comes to you with a 'D' average in school you can't fuck with him! Period." So, all you've got to do is show him that book and stand on our manifesto. 'Well, you know, I'm with you G but dig if you really about this here you going to have at least a 'C' average.' It's really simple, "you're supposed to be in school and telling someone else to go to school and if you're not doing that…" Well then, when my sons show them that in 'black and white' they can't even argue let alone recruit them. In effect, they're blown away from them because they realize that they've been exposed to the truth.

I'm not just telling you that you should abide by the manifesto of Growth and Development. I'm not just talking about Growth and Development because it sounds good. We live by that truth in my house. My family abides by the Growth and Development program. On June 13, 2011, my son Leviticus Bradley graduated valedictorian of his class at Whistler Elementary School; he was number one in his class. Furthermore, he received the Maple Park Overall Exemplary Student Award; Outstanding Academic Achievement Award from 34th Ward Alderman/ Chairman Carrie M. Austin; Lemuell Austin Foundation Academic Achievement Award; Excellence in Education Valedictorian Award from Mrs. Carla L. Diggs, Principal; Winner of the Chicago Public School System 18th District Writing Contest; Creative Publication Poetry Winner and the Young Authors Competition Award. Leviticus Bradley is an example of what is means to live by the code of ethics as expressed in our manifesto, 'Growth and Development.' ["Education is the passport to the future, for tomorrow belongs to those who prepare for it today."- Malcolm X]

We believe also in the ballot as opposed to the bullet. That belief is the reason why when we devised the political action organization, 21st Century VOTE, we were strategically priming young brothers and sisters who were coming of age in the 1990s to be prepared to vote in the 21st century. We also prepared them to get educated regardless if they failed. After all, if you learn from failure then you have acquired knowledge and that is education. It was mandatory for Gangster Disciples in the penitentiary to go school. All of us went into the joint as 'functionally illiterate' young adults; we could read and write very little but just enough- some of us not at all. A lot of us came out of the penitentiary educated and went on to become paralegals, entrepreneurs and everything else.

I applied the same code or rules of 'Growth and Development' to the work I did with Gery Chico on his mayoral campaign because every ethnic group has policies and principles, so-to-speak, to help them go from a negative to a positive. When you have the Hispanic community representing say about five percent in Chicago, okay, yet they get eleven to fourteen percent of the contracts in the city, something is wrong with that program but they have applied their rules and policies. When you see their communities being self contained, that's a code; for example, if you go into the Hispanic community you might not even see one single Chinese restaurant. You follow what I'm saying. You're not going to see an Arab corner grocery or some other ethnicity with a gas station in their community. Okay. When you go to a furniture store in their community, it is a Hispanic owned and operated furniture store. So, that is self-containment and that's part of their code; you follow what I'm saying. The Hispanic community believes in their principles and policies and then they become political.

So, my code of ethics is written under the manifesto, 'Growth and Development.' Everyone has principles and policies in place. I stand for 'Growth and Development,' that's what I believe and I don't run from it. In 1994, I was invited by Reverend Jesse Jackson to be a part of a delegation to meet with President Clinton- which also happened to be the first time I met Rahm [Emanuel]. We were gathered together to talk about that bogus crime bill or 'three strikes law,' which basically stated, 'three strikes and you're out.' For example, if an individual had two prior convictions he might end up with a twenty-five years to life sentence for shoplifting a pair of socks or taking a slice of pepperoni pizza from a group of kids [as was the case with Jerry Dewayne Williams in California]. We were also discussing bogus legislation that would give a five year sentence to someone convicted of having one gram of crack cocaine; yet, an individual would have to be caught with one hundred grams of powder cocaine to be given the same sentence. This one hundred to one ratio was clearly targeting individuals in urban areas of a lower socio-economic class. [In 2010, President Obama's Fair Sentencing Act narrowed the ratio from 100:1 to 18:1]. Okay and all of that let me know that the administration knew exactly who I was and why I was there. In meetings they might say, "Okay Gator, what do you think?" They didn't say, 'Mr. Bradley.' They didn't say, 'Wallace.' They called me, "Gator." The airlines knew that I was more than just another head to be counted on the flight to Washington, DC. And everyone knows that before you can even have a telephone conversation with the president of the United States, let alone meet with him in the Oval Office, that the FBI, the CIA and everybody else is going through everything about your present and your past, even down to who you loved last. Everything. They knew I was there as a former enforcer for Larry Hoover and it was still Gangster Disciples then, you follow me.

It has been a journey; I have evolved. Many have witnessed my growth; I have developed and now I am fifty-nine years old. It is my responsibility to pass down the wisdom I have gained from my experiences to my daughter, my granddaughter and my great-grandson. And along to my sons, I have to pass that down. I am a living example and I am passing down the spirit of *Growth and Development*.

During the mayoral debates I took my daughter and my granddaughter to the DuSable Museum [African American History Museum]. It was the first time that all of the mayoral candidates had been gathered together at once at DuSable to participate in a debate. The event was hosted by the Chicago Defender [Founded in 1905 by Robert Sengstacke Abbott, the Chicago Defender, became the nation's first black daily newspaper.] during black history month; February. The previous month there had been a debate at Trinity [Trinity United Church of Christ where the acclaimed Jeremiah Wright once served as pastor.] The situation in the church during the debate brought a lot of negative media attention to Carol Mosley Braun when she exhibited hostility and disrespect toward her fellow candidate Patricia Van Pelt-Watkins. [Carol Mosley Braun was the first black female United States Senator 1993-1999; United States Ambassador to New Zealand 1999-2001; candidate for the Democratic nomination in the 2004 United States Presidential election and candidate for mayor of Chicago in 2011.]

At the Trinity debate, Watkins made a statement about Braun's commitment to the African American community by saying that we don't need someone in office who had been "missing in action and lost somewhere for the last twenty years" to suddenly decide she wanted to be mayor [according to Fox Chicago news]. Braun was clearly angry and responded to Watkins by saying, "...the reason you didn't know where I was the last twenty years is because you were strung out on crack!" Watkins admitted that she had been a drug addict in her life but said that she's now sober, has a doctorate and runs a church. This debate wasn't the first time Carol had made a crack like that during the mayoral race. She did the same thing like three or four other times on various issues. It's like, 'Whoa wait a minute!' and hey baby it had gotten so wild that the blacks who could donate money to Carol's campaign had stopped giving her any. Her money got so tight due to dwindling support that she couldn't broadcast television spots she had produced. Fast-forward two months later to April [21st] and Carol needed the newly elected mayor, Rahm Emanuel, to headline a fundraiser to help her retire the debt from her campaign.

Moving along, my daughter and my granddaughter had seen all of this on television and now we were sitting on the front row at the DuSable debates. My granddaughter listened carefully to Carol speaking before she turned to me and said, "Granddad, you know I could someday become a United States Senator." Then she hears Pat speak who was a former drug addict and said, "Granddad, I see now that if I still fall short I can pick myself up and start all over again." My granddaughter sat there, watched and listened to both black female candidates for mayor.

When I looked back into the audience and I didn't see any children in the auditorium at DuSable Black History Museum to witness this historical debate I said to myself, 'Why is it that Operation Push didn't have a bus load of people here?' I also asked myself, 'Why is it that all of you adults who are in here can talk about how the young adults have to do something, have to be active and how we've got to pass the torch; yet, they did not bring their children or someone else's children?' Here at a black museum, during Black History Month, in a forum of mayoral candidates for the great city of Chicago. Furthermore, up until this point Rahm Emanuel hadn't come to a forum and this was the first forum he had ever attended in the black community- during the election. And the reason he came to the forum at DuSable is because [business woman and Indigo founder] Hermene Hartman was basically like, "You can't take me for granted. If I'm with you then this is what you have to do." Again, they're not paying attention that Hermene Hartman and I were wise enough to think about our grandchildren and our children and our great-grandkids. When they look back they'll be able to say, 'The reason this man is still the mayor twenty years later and doing the right things for all of us in the community is because of the right decisions made by people like Gator Bradley and Hermene Hartman.' And that's so profound because my generation had Malcolm X, we had Marvin Gaye and Rosa Parks. Our children don't have them to look back on, in their lifetime. Now they can look back on a former gang member, whose friend is Larry Hoover, who made a decision that we've got to better ourselves for our children.

So, on April 4th in the year 1995 I held a press conference after I lost the 3rd Ward aldermanic election to Dorothy Tillman subsequent to a runoff or special election. I had thirty-one percent of the votes to her forty-eight percent and she needed fifty percent to win outright. It was at that press conference when I made the public statement that I am no longer a Gangster Disciple. I said that I believe in and stand for the tenets of *Growth and Development*.

7 21ST CENTURY VOTE

The ideal of liberty demanded for its attainment powerful means, and these the Fifteenth Amendment gave him. The ballot, which before he had looked upon as a visible sign of freedom, he now regarded as the chief means of gaining and perfecting the liberty with which war had partially endowed him. And why not? Had not votes made war and emancipated millions? Had not votes enfranchised the freedmen? Was anything impossible to a power that had done all this? A million black men started with renewed zeal to vote themselves into the kingdom.

W.E.B. DuBois

Souls of Black Folk (1903)

Brother Larry Hoover is my friend and confidante. The manifestation of his vision of our going from Gangster Disciple to Growth and Development is evident. The man, Larry Hoover, went from being a negative to being a positive. We both believe that in order to change for the better and save our children we have to make it where the ballot is more important than the bullet. This realization is what brought about the conceptualization of 21st Century Vote- that was in the 90s- right before I met with President Bill Clinton in the Oval Office, which was in January of 1994.

The first time I ran for 3rd Ward Alderman was in 1991. I did this in order to test the fact and legitimacy of me having a pardon from former Governor Jim Thompson; he used to be a U.S. Attorney here in Chicago, crime was his platform. He granted me a pardon in 1990 and so I ran for office in 1991, to test the validity of that pardon. There's a law that restricts ex-felons from getting on the ballot; I would know the full legitimacy of my pardon if I could get on the ballot. Well, I ended up on the ballot. Out of nine people in the race for alderman I came in third place. After the election I went down to visit Larry Hoover at the Vienna Correctional Institution and he said, "Man, Gator. Man had you gotten with me we could've won that." I said, "Man, you know you're right." Then I added, "I was testing it to see if I was credible and legal with them to run." You see, it wasn't so much about me running as much as it was to make it where someone else who was an ex-convict who had changed their life around would have a right by law to run.

I ran on my own in 1991 but when I came back in 1995 I was running for 21st Century Vote. In that time, we had built a political and socially conscious organization and with the organization behind me I ended up in a run-off with Dorothy Tillman. Now that's when the government started to get busy. The U.S. Attorney in 1995 was James Burns; his Assistant U.S. Attorney was Ronald S. Safer. Between the two of them they broke all kinds of laws to try and destroy 21st Century Vote. These guys went so far as to come at Larry Hoover with a bogus wiretap. They did not have permission to bug people who went into the visiting booth or the visiting room to visit with Larry Hoover. Thereby, Larry Hoover and his visitors were all victims of illegal wire-tapping a crime committed against them by the government. The wiretaps were illegal and the tapes recorded during those visits were not sealed. Discussing those details would start to go off into another story and I'm just trying to give you a foundation, okay.

In 1994, Rahm Emmanuel- the same Rahm Emmanuel who ran for mayor of Chicago in the February 2011 election and won- was working with Bill Clinton in the White House and pushing for the passage of a crime bill that we now know was targeted toward African Americans and Hispanics. With two million people in penal institutions because of the laws, a million of them are African American men. In January of 1994, Reverend Jackson invited me to become a part of his delegation to go to the Oval Office to meet with President Clinton. He had a week long performance with the Oval Office to discuss the crime bill and other issues plaguing the African American community. Our meeting about the crime bill was scheduled to take place the day before he gave the State of the Union Address. The crime bill was targeting African American and Hispanic youth. It all was so bogus, for example, if I got caught with a bag of refer it would become a part of my permanent record; then, I wouldn't be able to get a Pell Grant to go to college because I got caught with drugs. Even if one time I made that mistake, I would be ruined for life with no chance for me to turn that back around. I met with the president and I spoke to Congress about this issue. If you look on my website you'll see the C-SPAN broadcast of me explaining the crime bill to Congress. Bill Cosby and a lot of other social and political activists were present.

Fast forward... Now Rahm Emmanuel was here running for Mayor of the City of Chicago and he was saying that he should be mayor because he is responsible for pushing a policy where they are supposed to be putting one hundred thousand police on the streets and yadda, yadda, yadda. Everyone was thinking, 'Now oh you're lockin' up all of our kin folks? And you're saying that gives you the right to be mayor?' I knew of Rahm before the mayoral race and during the race I supported the candidate who ran against him. And my candidate, Chico, just so happened not to be the black candidate who was the former United States Senator, Carol Mosley Braun.

The Gang Peace Summit was put together under United in Peace along with Larry Hoover. I have an interview on my website with Larry Hoover saying the same thing. Cornel West was supporting us during our Gang Peace Summits. Even Minister Louis Farrakhan, Jesse Jackson and Ben Chavis- when he was with the NAACP- were part the Gang Peace Summit initiatives. United in Peace has done a lot to address gang violence and gang peace. An early initiative was to facilitate gang peace for the purpose of getting people out to vote. In the projects- the Robert Taylor Homes and the other projects- each one has a polling place there where you can go to vote but they couldn't be crossed because of gang lines.

Let's say I'm in Building Two, okay, and my precinct where I have to go and vote is in Building One. Well, Building Two is Gangster Disciples and Building One is Black Disciples- that's going to present a problem for me going to the poll. So when we put the Gang Peace Summit together I mean it was so tight where an individual from another organization couldn't pick up a gun and shoot anybody without first bringing that concern to a governing body. Even to the point if I'm a GD and the other guy is a BD, okay, but my woman leaves me and goes to hook up with him and I want to fight him over her, I couldn't do that.

Larry Hoover asked me to be his 'Enforcer for Peace.' He addressed me and all the other gang leaders saying, "See man, we've got to save our children." At the time we were in the '90s and we were dealing with the mind so we decided on 21st Century Vote; preparing individuals to vote in the 21st century. Okay, so all of them- and I'm talking all the way to the Vienna Correctional Facility- got their permission from all the gang leaders in order to put their signs on this one button with two hands cupped together with the writing saying, United in Peace. So, it was broken down between the five point and the six point- I'm talking about the stars- the five point and the six point star. Okay, that's the difference between Folks and Peoples. The

Folks have the six point star and the Peoples have the five point star. So our thing was everyone knew I had the blessing of Larry and the GDs were the biggest gang in the city. The Gangster Disciples were more organized and structured than any of the other organizations. We gathered together protesters just to give our people a chance to walk downtown and be seen. We had ten thousand of them march downtown to stop a school strike. This is the power that we had.

In 1993, everybody was excited about seeing Carol Moseley Braun become the first African American woman to go the U.S. Senate and we wanted to help. So, we made it where okay, everybody that was going to vote had a right to go across all lines to voting polls. We made it where if you want to go to school you have the right to cross gang territory during school hours- and all that stuff- to go to school. The rule was that nobody could pick up a pistol and shoot another person- for any reason- without first bringing their concerns to the table. Now just like I was the enforcer for peace for Larry, Jeff [Fort, co-founder of the Black P. Stone Nation and founder of the El Rukns] had someone who was that way for him. The Four Corners [the Four Corner Hustlers] had to have somebody who was that way for them. So we all worked together. If there was a problem then all we needed was the address where that problem might be, then we'd find out what organization was represented at that address. Each organization had someone who was similar to me, an enforcer for peace; however, Larry was the most vocal leader. You have to understand this; all the other gang leaders out there have been in and out of the penitentiary. Larry has never been in and out, he has always been in. So he watched a lot of those guys, he stopped a lot of them from getting raped and everything else. They respected him because he is telling them, "Hey man ain't no opposition in here we're all locked up in this penitentiary."

At this time Carol can't get elected to the senate; now here it is she ran for mayor and Rahm also ran for mayor. We have gone from 1994 to 2011. I know Carol personally from when she was a state representative. My wife knew her niece, there were buddies. So, it wasn't strange to see Carol in the neighborhood; you know she's from the 'low end.' She was real personal, it was personal. Carol even had me to come speak before a United States Senate Committee that she was chairman of dealing with gangster rap- me and Snoop Dogg. When she was in the United States Senate she never closed the door to me. Anytime I came there I was welcome to come up to her office.

Helping to get Barack Obama elected as President of the United States was a learning experience for me. Obama winning the presidency was the manifestation of 21st Century Vote. The individuals who were young adults and former gang bangers in the 90s when the organization was formed to educate and motivate to vote are now adults. It was already engrained in their minds that someday we might be able to elect a president because we helped elect a United States Senator. And now Barack Obama is elected president. So everyone is asking what ever happened to 21st century vote? 21st century vote has evolved from being a concept. It has evolved from an organization with members who were once young gang bangers and gang members to an organization of responsible adults, the same individuals with a new mindset.

8 CONSENSUS CANDIDATE

The crisis in black leadership can be remedied only if we candidly confront its existence. We need national forums to reflect, discuss, and plan how to best respond. It is neither a matter of a new Messiah figure emerging, nor of another organization appearing on the scene. Rather it is a matter of grasping the structural and institutional processes that have disfigured, deformed, and devastated black America such that the resources for nurturing collective and critical consciousness, moral commitment, and courageous engagement are vastly underdeveloped. We need serious strategic and tactical thinking about how to create new models of leadership and forge the kind of persons to actualize these models.

Cornel West
Race Matters (1993)

November 2010, Danny Davis [United States Representative] and Reverend Meeks [James T. Meeks, Illinois State Senator] announced their candidacy for mayor. A lot of us in the city- particularly in the black community- agreed that we needed to band together and get behind one of the candidates. We held a meeting of aldermen, businessmen and other members of the community- and the city- to vote on what they called a 'consensus candidate.' In other words, we gathered to decide on one person for us to rally behind collectively in order to give them the best chance at winning the mayoral election.

We started to weigh the odds; like, Meeks had twenty thousand members of his church. As for Danny Davis, of the nineteen aldermen there were fifteen of them who would go with him; so, that means he had fifteen wards plus several political organizations that would back him. Now Carol, Carol didn't have anything or at least very little by comparison. Several members of the business community came forward and said they were willing to give Carol and Meeks their money. Well, Meeks said, 'I'm going to drop out of the race because I don't have fifteen wards plus several political organizations with anywhere from seven to ten thousand voters that they can call on just like that.' Carol shouted out, 'Well ain't nobody going to bully me out of the race! I'm staying in the race; I'm staying in the race.' They said okay but Meeks dropped out anyway. So, then there's Danny Davis. Danny Davis went to the money folks then said, 'Okay, I'm out here and I have the experience. I used to be a city alderman; I was elected Cook County Commissioner; I'm a congressman; I know power brokers from here to DC; and, I ran for mayor before so I know not to make the same mistakes.' Even with all of his experience and credentials the business community didn't go with Davis; they still pushed Carol.

Later we found out that a lot of politicians and members of the business community were pushing Carol because she was the weaker candidate. Silently, they were behind Rahm Emmanuel- you follow what I'm saying- just to get what they could for themselves and not for the community. Now Hermene and I have been in this game since 1988. We were with Jackson when he ran for president and we were on certain committees where we saw all the businessmen in action- you know the money folks- and we know the games they play, to make a long story short. Therefore, we realized that we couldn't play the game the same way. So, that's the reason why when they made the decision to go with Carol, Carol was cocked, ok, 'I'm it ah ah ah…'

Earlier during our discussions for this book Dr. SaFiya asked me the question if I thought Carol's remark to Watkins at DuSable was just an arrogant or an ignorant outburst. Well, an ignorant outburst is when you say some dumb shit because you were drunk-you follow what I'm saying- and really don't have what is known in academia as education, awareness or knowledge. Well, when you have been a United States Senator and an Ambassador- you follow what I'm saying- you're supposed to have humility and diplomacy for the positions that you carry and character because of the fact that you were elected. You don't make irresponsible remarks; that's not an ignorant outburst, that's being a damn fool. The first time individuals might let it slide but when you do it the second time, we're like, "Whoooa!" Then when you do it a third time that's when people who were with you start backing away from you. Why? Because they know people say that, 'birds of a feather flock together' and they don't want to get caught up because of association with you. So, that left the black community with nothing.

Now that Carol had cut her own tail with the media fiascos and her declining support, Rahm saw his opportunity to make inroads into the black community-even though they knew he didn't care anything about black folk. He realized that he had become a congressman by securing votes from the very same people who he was trying to now destroy. These people were union folk and the mob, the white mob- you follow me- and black folk. Listen to what I'm getting ready to tell you- and Bobby Rush should have thought about everything I'm getting ready to say. Why? Bobby Rush knows about the kinds of votes Rahm made while he was in congress. Rush, Jackson, Jr., and Davis knew he voted against everything that the Congressional Black Caucus was putting down and they know that Rahm kept the black leaders away from coming to meet with President Obama because he was the Chief of Staff. Bobby knew this, Jesse Jr. knew this, Danny Davis knew this and they didn't inform the black community until damn near a week before the elections. They knew that this man voted one hundred twenty eight times, as a Democrat, against programs that were coming to the African American community even a program that was coming to Chicago State University. When Rahm announced that he was going to run all they had to do was inform the community from that day of who this guy really was and they didn't do it.

The thing is this, for whatever reason they didn't inform the public of Rahm's track record it was their responsibility to make the people aware of their firsthand knowledge about whom this individual was. So, when they didn't and the people saw these same leaders pushing Carol it made the black electors say, 'Damn! What the fuck is really happening?!' If you all knew this man was anti-black, anti-immigrants and anti- working class people why you didn't tell us? There you all are right there pushing a candidate, saying that you're representing her and they're like, 'Oh shit, y'all ain't representing us!' So, when Hermene made that move with Rahm and I made the move with Chico it made them gravitate toward us. It made them say, 'well we're not going to waste our vote with Carol.' Ok. If there is going to be a run-off then let our folk either be with the winner or at least be a part of the run-off when they have they have the final showdown. Subsequently, that's when you see Rahm was number one and Chico was number two; the other guy del Valle [City Clerk, Miguel del Valle] was number three and Carol was number four. Carol got nine percent of the vote- fifty thousand votes.

When the black community saw that their leaders didn't really inform them you know it made everyone say, "Well who am I voting for? Now you're telling me that this man is damn near worse than the 'Grinch who stole Christmas.' Man what am I going to do?" The people were thinking, 'Danny Davis I depend on you and Bobby Rush I depend on you to let me know what's up.' They were confused because of the feeling that, 'Hey I'm following you; y'all meet up with Carol and then y'all tell us we ain't supporting the consensus candidate.' So, the thing is this baby, none of the black aldermen came out publicly to show support for Rahm or Chico. You hear what I'm telling you? Okay, none of them. So, we had to assume some form of leadership by virtue of our focus. We had to take on the responsibility to make a move and say to the people, 'Hey look, please come out and vote and if you're going to vote make sure that your vote is being counted.' First of all, if the attendees at that 'consensus' meeting would have pushed Danny Davis for mayor he would have locked the city up as far as the black vote. The reason is because the Westside and the Southside would have come together to support Davis. Plus, finally they would have been giving the Westside their just due. The Westside was mad when the major players pushed Carol instead of Danny Davis. They said, 'Look Southside you all have had a black mayor, you all have had two United States Senators and you all have had two candidates for president. And the Westside has always come out in numbers to support the Southside's candidates.' They were understandably perturbed thinking, 'Now we have a qualified candidate for mayor and you all have the nerve to come and tell us that you're not going to support him?!'

9 POWER PLAYS

If [Dr.] Martin Luther King Jr. were to return miraculously to Chicago, some forty years after bringing his Freedom Movement to the city, he would be saddened to discover that the same issues on which he originally focused still produced stark patterns of racial inequality, segregation, and poverty.

Michelle Alexander
The New Jim Crow: Mass Incarceration in the Age of Colorblindness (2010)

People from all over Chicago could be heard voicing their opinions. Even though a lot of us in the African American community felt like Rahm Emmanuel shouldn't have been elected mayor, he was elected mayor. The wisest thing that happened as a part of his being elected is that Hermene Hartman came out and she endorsed Rahm Emmanuel.

I know Hermene well because we were with Reverend James T. Meeks when he announced that he was going to run for Mayor of Chicago. When Reverend Meeks dropped out of the race other leaders like Jesse Jackson, Danny Davis, the whole enchilada of middle class African Americans- you know the academicians and the business folks- they all pushed Carol Moseley Braun for mayor. Hermene and I saw that was a disaster because we knew we couldn't put everything in one basket. So, I endorsed Gery Chico, former Chief of Staff to Mayor Richard M. Daley and Chicago Public Schools Board President; she endorsed Rahm Emanuel, former White House Chief of Staff to President Barack Obama. We strategically endorsed each of the leading candidates so that the African American urban agenda would become a necessary part of any incoming mayor's agenda.

So, you've got three different candidates strongly backed by members of the African American community.

In order for our agenda to be included with whomever would become mayor we had to have someone in every camp; that's the lesson that was learned after Barack Obama got elected. We all realized that the fatal mistake we made is that we didn't have an urban agenda before all the presidential candidates whether they were Republican or Democrat. We didn't have our agenda before candidates challenging them and forcing them to where they had to make a determination before anyone cast a vote. So, because the African American community didn't do that every other group had their agendas presented- upfront, first and foremost- requiring that all the presidential candidates had to make a decision. Other communities made it a point to have their voices heard whether it was the lesbian and gay or LGBT community; whether it was the Hispanic community with the immigration laws; whether it was business interests or exclusively women's interests; these communities put their agendas before all of the presidential candidates. However, we as African Americans failed to put our agendas before all the presidential candidates; we just felt that since Barack Obama was an African American and his wife was an African American it should be natural that our agendas would be his concerns. ["I think that we should push the president. This president runs from race like a black man runs from a cop. What we have to do is ask Mr. Obama to stand up and use his bully pulpit to help us. He is loathe to speak about race." -Michael Eric Dyson, 2010]

Well, now we know that the African American agenda wasn't a concern or a priority because we didn't present our agenda to Obama; and, now that he's president he doesn't even have to really deal with our agenda. We must hold ourselves accountable for moves we did not make and factors we had taken for granted. As a result, when the Obama Administration put out its budget we see that the first thing he's cutting is programs that affect our community. Now you see that immigrant issues are being discussed with Obama pushing for The DREAM Act- Development, Relief and Education for Alien Minors- that would provide for undocumented immigrants. The Dream Act says for example, that if an undocumented immigrant graduates from high school here or resides in the U.S. for so many years before the bill is passed they can be given permanent residency and undocumented immigrants can receive full scholarships to cover tuition at public and private colleges- among other things. But for some reason it almost doesn't apply to the Haitians- you follow me, okay.

Now we see where this president actively addressed the lesbian and gay agenda by successfully pushing to end the "Don't ask, don't tell" (DADT) policy on homosexuals who are serving in the United States military. DADT barred individuals from openly disclosing their sexual orientation or serving if they demonstrated a "propensity or intent to engage in homosexual acts;" it also said that their military superiors could not have them investigated- among other things. You know; so, their concerns were a part of the agenda from the very beginning.

When we say, "Hey man this is what you have to do to help stop the killing in our communities and we need better jobs and we need better education in our community..." They say, "Well Barack you can't go do that because them niggas can't have you looking so black;" only because it wasn't part of the agenda. So, what I'm saying, now with Rahm being there or if Chico had been there or if Carol had become the mayor our agenda would be addressed because we made it a part of their agenda- you follow what I'm saying- we learned from our mistake in the election of Barack Obama.

Whatever my opinion might have been of Rahm becoming mayor doesn't matter because the fact is, he's now mayor of Chicago. It is satisfactory enough to see him go to Hermene Hartman and say, "thank you." She helped him garner the support of the African American community; he won with the black vote. Now, he has won with the black vote and he's aware that he has to bring something back to the black community because he signed on to something that Hermene brought to him. She brought him an agenda that's going to 'help you not only get elected but to help you get re-elected if you stay true to this agenda.'

As it regards Chico's campaign, even though Chico had accepted my endorsement members of his campaign staff were racially profiling me. Had they arrived at the same conclusion Hermene was proposing then he would have had people in the black community showing that Chico's signing on to the agenda for all of us to be included and governed by a mayor who is the mayor of all people, an inclusive mayor. What I mean by that is this, when I produced my commercial for Chico, I did it out of my own pocket because I had it in black and white that he was sincere about the re-entry program to help ex-felons. The re-entry program would help ex-felons who can qualify for a job to secure employment and start their life over again; pretty much like the second chance program that Congressman Danny Davis had passed into law and signed by former President Bush. Therefore, our agenda was being addressed by two of the mayoral candidates, you follow me. To keep it real with you, I don't know that Carol had signed off on either one of those ex-felon initiatives because she didn't make it publicly known or at least acknowledge that, 'Hey I'm for ex-felons getting better jobs.'

Another issue, African Americans may represent thirty-five to maybe forty percent of the city of Chicago; yet, they were only getting three percent of city contracts. Hermene, being in the business arena, clearly helped to justify her supporting Rahm; again, with her endorsement he signed on to the fact that one of the first things he would do is make sure that African Americans and other minorities were both getting their fair share of city contracts. In other words, instead of it just being said that so many minorities should get city contracts and then they (all 'minorities' other than African Americans) end up getting contracts or being front companies; the city would have make sure that all minorities 'and' African Americans got their fair share of city contracts. You follow what I'm saying; that's the difference. Rahm was amenable to that; so, now the city is looking like, 'Jesse and everybody else went with Carol.' Well, Carol is out of there and if she is out of there and she didn't sign on to the issue of ex-felons or city contracts, then she really doesn't have anything coming. That's how they played it.

The first thing that Rahm did when he won was to call Gery Chico who was the second runner up in the mayoral race. They agreed that Chico was going to come out and say, 'Hey, I'm supporting Rahm and I want everybody to support me in supporting this man; he's our next mayor.' Rahm, in his new position as mayor of Chicago had planned to go after Alderman [Ed] Burke who is considered Chicago's "most powerful alderman." [Burke was first elected in 1969 to his seat in the 14th Ward. He is currently the longest serving alderman to a single ward in Chicago's history. His father Joseph Burke had been elected 14th Ward Alderman in 1953.] Specifically, Rahm intended to go after him over the Finance Committee where he controls a 1.3 million dollar payroll account for alderman which is funded by tax-payers. Rahm basically said, 'When I get in I'm going to take your finance committee and get rid of your security guards.' [It had been reported in the media that Rahm blamed Burke for laying the groundwork for his residency to be challenged as a potential stalemate to his mayoral candidacy.] Alderman Burke is Chico's mentor; so, when Chico went and met with Rahm he asked him to back up off of Burke, because that's in his interest.

Hermene and I both see that we have to be concerned about our interests; and, there is that part of our egos that cares what someone might say about us. So, that decision was a serious growing pain [to back Rahm Emanuel and

Gery Chico]. We were just like two birds; our parents know that we can fly, all they have to do is kick our ass, kick us off the gotdamn fence and we're either going to fall to the ground or we're going to flap our wings like say, 'Damn!' You follow what I'm saying? So, that's what we did, we got off the fence and flew. Recently, one morning I was talking with Hermene and let it be known that I don't have any problem with reaching out to Rahm whether it's through her to say, "Hey, here's my program about public safety and helping to stop the killing in our communities," or something else. He may say, 'Hey, hey, Hermene,' and Hermene might tell him, 'Hey, Gator was out there as a leader, he made a statement and he paid for the commercial not thru Gery Chico but he did it on his own.' So, that in fact, see, makes me participatory player in the game instead of being just a participant as a voter. Hermene will be showing Rahm by our introduction that, hey, the same way he reached out to Burke and just like he reached out to Gery Chico- you follow what I'm saying- 'You [Rahm Emanuel] will have to reach out to Mr. Bradley too and say I would like to talk with you about your concerns.' The clever part is that he's going to already know my concerns- you follow what I'm saying- she's going to be letting him know that she can go to Mr. Bradley and bring him in because his concerns about public safety, education, jobs and fair contracts for everyone in the city of Chicago are the same.

There is so much that goes into campaigning. Dealing with these campaigns, you know, your brain will go dead on you and all these late hours will slap you upside the head and knock you out. By the time elections ended I went into a 'social coma.'

Rhymefest ['El' Che Smith] ended up in a run-off in April against incumbent, Alderman [Willie] Cochran for the 20th Ward alderman seat. When I saw him he said, "Man, Gator I'm proud of you." "Look," I told him, "dude I'm proud of you too." In the 90s he was a part of the group of individuals form the street who we were motivating to go from a negative to a positive, and he got caught up too. We reached out to them like, "You all have talent, get up from out of here making this muthafuckin' dope and I better not catch you!" When I ran for alderman it was to let them know that some day they could run for alderman too. Now look at Rhymefest, he had made some mistakes in his past- nobody's perfect- but he's gone from a negative to a positive. Rhymefest was running for alderman and placing on the Hip Hop community their responsibilities to continue the positive movement that they had when they got out there for Barack Obama, it doesn't stop. The Hip Hop community has to be socially conscious activists just like Stevie Wonder, just like Marvin Gaye- you follow what I'm saying- just like Curtis Mayfield, just like Mahalia Jackson. Yeah, he was in the run-off. My partner Harold [Hal] Baskin of the 16th ward was also in a run-off. He had been a part of the gang summits that we did back in the day. As a matter of fact, he was one of the gang leaders we honored at a celebration- I think it was- where we were giving out awards to the gang leaders who were working to help stop the violence in the 90s. We both ran in 1995 and ended up in a run-off in our respective wards. The headlines read that there were two gang leaders in a run-off in the special election; but, we lost because Daley supported Dorothy Tillman and he supported the candidate that Harold was running against. So, when Daley dropped out he came back again.

[Roderick] Sawyer was in the run-off for the 6th Ward. Mayor [Eugene] Sawyer- his father- was my lawyer in 1995 when I ran for office; but, it was Roderick Sawyer and his father Mayor Sawyer who went to the Illinois Prison Review Board to speak on Larry Hoover's behalf to try to get him paroled. That was is in the 90s.

To be silent would have meant that Hermene Hartman and I never would have had that conversation to bring something out of nothing. If I was silent that conversation wouldn't have happened. When I saw Rahm Emanuel winning or when I saw how he won; and, when I got a call to confirm how he won and how he tried to make amends for all the wrongs that he did to the black community; I said, "I will never be silent even in death." I have performed the works where individuals can go back and say, 'Man this is what Gator did, this is what we've got to do,' it's like we have to carry it on to the next level. People may be on rocket ships but they'll say, 'man we got to act like we tryin' to get somewhere higher.' I will not be foolish but I will not be silent.

The mayoral elections are long over but my agenda is the same as before, the same as it always has been. My agenda is all about public safety, education, jobs, fairness in jobs and the awarding of city contracts. My purpose now is showing what Growth and Development is all about. You know, you grow and you develop and you become a better person. Someone must continue to make it where our children and grandchildren can cut into this society and not be cut out of society because of whom they are or who their parents were. We're in the 21st Century now, alright, they have made everything so easy and accessible to the point that they can cut our children out very easily. You follow what I'm saying?

Effecting change, being heard and making a difference is like what we have witnessed taking place over in Egypt. Alright, you see how the young adults in Egypt have come out and said we no longer want the government that we had in place for thirty years. Then you see what has happened over in Wisconsin right here in the United States where the republican governor was saying that he's going to cut back on the unions and destroy the unions to the point that fifty-thousand people marched on the state's capitol. You had the democratic state senators and house members coming over here in Illinois so they wouldn't be arrested in Wisconsin because they wouldn't have to go to a meeting. You follow what I'm saying? So, the fact is that in all cases they were fighting for their issues and concerns. When their issues and concerns get addressed if there's no black person at that table saying, 'Well, I want to make sure not just the Polish or the Irish or the Jewish or the Hispanic union workers get something I want to make sure Blacks get something too!' If we are not represented at the table then our concerns are overlooked.

It is very important to me to do what I can to further what Hermene Hartman and I were talking about. I have to set a road map; so, even if we die it won't become some, 'Keep Hope Alive' speech. There will be a road map to be followed because as we did what we did, we were also in the position to teach why we did it; so, that our children will know that this is how it's to be done.

10 BOGEYMAN

Rescue me, LORD, from evildoers; protect me from the violent, who devise evil plans in their hearts and stir up war every day. They make their tongues as sharp as a serpent's; the poison of vipers is on their lips.

Keep me safe, LORD, from the hands of the wicked; protect me from the violent, who devise ways to trip my feet. The arrogant have hidden a snare for me; they have spread out the cords of their net and have set traps for me along my path.

I say to the LORD, "You are my God." Hear, LORD, my cry for mercy. Sovereign LORD, my strong deliverer, you shield my head in the day of battle. Do not grant the wicked their desires, LORD; do not let their plans succeed.

Those who surround me proudly rear their heads; may the mischief of their lips engulf them. May burning coals fall on them; may they be thrown into the fire, into miry pits, never to rise. May slanderers not be established in the land; may disaster hunt down the violent. I know that the LORD secures justice for the poor and upholds the cause of the needy. Surely the righteous will praise your name, and the upright will live in your presence.

Psalm 140

New International Version of the Holy Bible

I have what they call a 'Bogeyman effect' or a 'Nicodemus effect' on some people in my professional life. Individuals come to me in the darkness of the night and they say, "Gator we need your support, we need somebody to scream and say we ought to have a right to get the contracts;" and, then when they get them they don't even want to hire me as a consultant. You follow what I'm saying? Okay, so when their children get caught up or their daughter is caught up with a guy who is in the drug game and all that- for example- then they come to me and ask, "Gator can you call somebody?" All I do is ask, "What's his name? You got a phone number? Ok, where's he at? What organization is he in?" Next, I call the leader of that organization and then I call the individual in question on his phone and say, "Man look, don't mess with that young lady there. Whatever you do it stops now; not in that house." But these individuals don't want to come out publicly and say we reached out to Gator to help us.

So, I take all that in stride because I know God watches over righteous folks and remain humble in my spirit, I know I'm going to protected. For this reason, the one prayer that I constantly pray to God is Psalms 140. That's my whole thing you know, it's like this here, they love to know that I'm around, it's like they hate for people to see me coming to them, okay, but when I leave they're glad to say, "Hey dig, I know Gator. I can get up with Gator;" or, "You know if you got a problem I can get up with Gator…" so they can be the one to say that they're the bridge to Gator. I take it for what it is. I just keep on stepping.

I love the game of politics! I love it, I love it. Oh now as far as the little sitcoms go, I love watching 'The Game' too. Seriously though, wow, I love politics. There's no one thing in particular that I love the most, I love the game; but, I can say that the campaign that I learned the most from was Jess Jackson's 1988 presidential campaign.

Of all my experiences in political arena, I'll say the 2011 mayoral campaign for Chico was real difficult because his campaign staff had racially profiled me and that may have been why he lost. It was difficult because even though I knew what they were doing I felt that he was a genuine candidate. It was difficult for me to the point that I had to pay out of my own pocket and do that commercial and it was for the betterment of their candidate. Now had he won they would have tried to make sure that I could not get anywhere near the man or even close to that administration. So, that was a rough one.

Chico and I were cool, we had a good professional relationship; and, I felt we were cool enough for him to tell his staff, 'Hey, look I appointed this man duties in my campaign.' I didn't see that kind of solid support coming from him; but, I was out there so I had to make the best of what I had out there. That's the reason why when Hermene made her move to back Rahm it was so wonderful. She made it where we as a people can't be denied that we had something to do with the making of the mayor. If Chico would have gotten in there it would have been damn near hard for me to show except that I was able to document it, what I was doing. When you look at my webpage you'll see how I was documenting shit that I was doing for his campaign.

Almost as soon as Chico accepted my endorsement all the little ministers started gathering around him trying make me be more of a bogeyman than anything else. They were trying to say Gator is the bogeyman and you all need us to do this or that in order to cover what you all are doing- and they couldn't do anything. So this election was a hard one; but, I have no regrets. I have no regrets at all about it.

When I made the decision to go with Chico- even though I knew his staff was racist- people were like, 'Gator that was the best thing you could've done because it let it be known that we are not a monolithic voting base. You making that move and endorsing Chico- instead of just standing next to him as if to be some type of joking negro-made it where we had options other than to rally all around Carol because we had put everything into her. Then when Hermene did what she did it shot my stock up even more.

I think it's true when some people say that you can judge the quality of a person's life by the friends and enemies they make. There's a saying that I apply to myself and that is, 'in the game of politics there are no prominent friends and no prominent enemies; only prominent interests.'

The happiest day of my career in politics was when I helped Jerry Butler to get elected as a Cook County Board Commissioner. He had brought me on board to work as his administrative assistant. I would also have to say that one of the happiest days of my career was when I got my pardon from Governor Thompson in 1990; because, my mother had asked me to do this as she was dying from cancer.

On the other hand, I think the saddest part of my career is when I lost the election to Dorothy Tillman because of the way the media had played a statement that I made. They claimed that I was trying to steal the votes when in actuality I had gone to the gym [polling place] because the young adults who were helping me to run for office were there crying and shouting, "Oh Mr. Bradley they are trying to steal your votes. They are trying to steal your votes." All while the police were standing right out there, the gangs had locked the gym so no one could take the votes out of there.

When I pulled up to the polling place the media gathered all around me. They said, "Gator well you're a Gangster Disciple Enforcer. You're the Gangster Disciple this and Gangster Disciple that." Now this happened before I knew the workings of the media and I said, "Ok, for the sake of argument I'm a Gangster Disciple who's trying to help people stop from killing one another and trying to show them that they have a right to justice and they are allowed to vote." I went on to say, "… and if I'm a Gangster Disciple, I'm not here fighting over any drug territory, I'm here fighting for them to have a right to make sure that they're votes are protected."

The media edited the prefix and the suffix of that whole interview and all they played was, "I'm a Gangster Disciple." They wrote about it and put it on televised news that Gator said Gangster Disciple and talked about all of them out there killing everybody up. The media successfully scared the seniors with this Bogeyman they made me out to be and I lost the election behind that statement broadcast out of context. The media fiasco outside of the gym and what resulted was the saddest day of my political career because I felt like I should have been alderman or at the very least quoted correctly. ["The media is the most powerful entity on the earth. They have the power to make the innocent guilty and to make the guilty innocent, and that's power. Because they control the minds of the masses."- Malcolm X]

My first experience with being misquoted and taken out of context in the media is the reason why I believe that for Carol to do what she had done- by disrespecting Watkins and blasting other people- was inexcusable because she had gained public trust; she was more intelligent or prepared even than I was. Carol knew about the media. And even though I was glad to have my own camera there because I was able to go on and show my entire statement; the media still had the power to edit what I said and play it out to more people than I could because YouTube wasn't around then. When you look on my webpage you'll see where I was able to go grab other news items and put everything together on the one page because I realized that the media was doing an in-depth investigation of me. I was able to post statements and video that I made and to place media coverage all together side by side on my page to show anyone exactly what I was saying. You can see footage there of me and Dorothy Tillman being interviewed during the debates. Just think of how things might be different if I had YouTube back then.

I was blown away when I first learned about YouTube. One of my sons told me, "You know dad, we've been keeping up with you through YouTube and Google and we saw you speaking down in front of City Hall." Then they pulled up the video and showed me, that blew me the fuck away because I realized that I was being watched globally! Subsequently, that's why that webpage that I put together is almost like a DVD of the book that you're reading now. Everybody can say they did what they did what they did but when you show what you did and how and where you did it, that's on another level.

When I'm on the news and I'm talking I know that's being edited. However, when I watch the same interview online, if I talked for three minutes I see the whole three minute conversation and the reaction from it. For example, when I spoke to Congress and it was aired on C-Span, no one could tell me that I wasn't getting respect from all of our leaders; especially, when I see them stand up and applaud me. I know, for example, that if we would not have gotten that picture of me standing in the Oval Office with the president some people might try to argue the fact that I was there. Because of that single picture no one will ever be able to say that, 'he's never been to the Oval Office.'

The Autobiography of Wallace Gator Bradley, Urban Translator

I have to say I'm blessed to be alive and have common sense in the 21st century. I have to thank the young adults, including my children, for making me aware of the power of what they've got access to and knowledge of. I'm learning from my kids as much as they are learning from me. I can say how I felt when I saw myself on YouTube, Google, blogs, websites, social media and other ways all over the Internet in a three letter word, 'W-O-W.'

11 URBAN TRANSLATOR

I realized that they could take everything from me except my mind and my heart. They could not take those things. Those things I still had control over. And I decided not to give them away.

Nelson Mandela

The choices we make about the lives we live determine the kinds of legacies we leave.

Tavis Smiley
The Other Wes Moore: One name, Two Fates (2010)

The Autobiography of Wallace Gator Bradley, Urban Translator

I am an Urban Translator, it is a profession that I created and I legitimated when I achieved my first milestone as an Urban Translator in Aaron Patterson's civil rights lawsuit against Jon Burge. In this capacity I act as a liaison between my client and the courtroom, attorneys and the media. My primary function as an Urban Translator is speaking to individuals in a language that they can understand. In other words, let me speak this to you in our language and then break it down to you in your language so you can understand- now we all understand.

In 2003, Patterson was found innocent and pardoned from Death Row by Illinois Governor [George] Ryan after it was determined that Patterson's confessions were brutally tortured out of him by Burge. As you already know, I'm a former Gangster Disciple. Well, Aaron Patterson was once a leader of the Black Stone Rangers, we once were enemies. In 2007- despite our gang pasts- we united together when I served as Urban Translator in his lawsuit against Jon Burge which ended with a five million dollar settlement. At the same time we went out and broke into the campaign to help Gery Chico get elected mayor, Jon Burge was found guilty for torturing individuals and sentenced to four and a half years. Burge was only given four and a half years because the conspiracy was so deep. He couldn't get charged for the torture because the court claimed that the statute of limitations had passed on the torture but the Attorney General did make a move to take his pension back- a move was put in to sue.

As Urban Translator in the Patterson case and in my everyday stance against police brutality and for the rights of people all I'm saying is everybody has a right to a fair trial. Everybody has the right to go after an individual who tortures people but the powers that be feel like they don't understand what we're saying. So, we say well it's all a play of words. I didn't create a profession where anyone can tell me what I can't be paid and I proved this when I had to sue Aaron Patterson. I represented him in his case against Jon Burge for torture and then he refused to pay me for my services rendered. Triumphantly, I won a settlement in my case against Patterson. When I won my suit to be paid for services rendered it made my profession, it made what I do, a real profession because I'm getting paid for my time.

I am currently working as Urban Translator in case for Melvin Jones who was also one of Jon Burge's torture victims. We're in the process of trying to sue the city because they conspired to cover up the torture that Jon Burge did not only Patterson and Jones but to a thousand people. This case is going to be so unique, we've got John Marshall Law School and we've got this attorney named

Sam Adams, Jr. Sam Adams, Jr. is a young brother; he defended R. Kelly and he represented Blagojevich. His father, Sam Adams, Sr. is also an attorney.

Adams, Sr. partnered with the pioneering civil rights attorney R. Eugene Pincham on cases. [Pincham also served as judge of the Circuit Court of Cook County and justice of the Appellate Court of Illinois.] Once they had a client with twenty-four federal charges against him and got it knocked down to one charge; he was acquitted of twenty-three charges and they asked for another trial. Adams, Sr. and Pincham were partners in a law firm that was helping a lot of the guys who belonged to different street organizations. Sam Adams, Jr. is going to be assisting me [and at John Marshall Law School] in suing the city.

Okay, now I'm going to give you a little more background information on Melvin Jones. Melvin Jones was a strong witness against Jon Burge and that's how Burge was finally convicted. Melvin Jones was tortured by Jon Burge and several police officers in an effort to get him to commit to a murder and he wouldn't commit to the murder. After they had tortured him by putting a cattle prod or stun gun on his nuts and everything else, the same way like they did the Wilson boys, they came back and re-arrested him then framed him for the murder. R. Eugene

Pincham was serving as the appellate court judge on this trial. He saw clearly that Jones had been framed and threw the case out after the man had been locked up for eight years. Pincham got Jones a new trial. Melvin Jones had to go back and pick another twelve members of the jury and he beat the case straight out because they had framed him. Now that Burge has been found guilty of torture Jones got a new statute of limitations- against conspiracy, against the city- and I am his urban translator.

In addition to being an Urban Translator I am a volunteer for different causes, organizations and events. I volunteer so much that they've taken the 'H' out of hope for me. That's why I get mad when individuals feel like I shouldn't have the right to get paid for my services. I feel like man I have volunteered and helped so many people to get elected, I'm volunteering here and there; and, when people call and ask me to help them I'm volunteering then. I volunteer for a lot of social and political organizational and individual efforts. ["Service to others is the rent you pay for your room here on earth."- Muhammad Ali]

I could never retire from social or political activism, for that reason I want to break into the speaking circuit. Activism is something that needs to be taught. I'm saying this because every Black History Month our black leaders in academia- whether it's in finance or education- never mention Elijah Muhammad. And he was a great leader because he taught us to be for self as a people.

Unfortunately, they omit Elijah Muhammad from lectures about history and discussions about politics and prosperity because they simply do not want our children to know about such a revolutionary black consciousness in America. They don't want them to know about the power of Black Wall Street in Tulsa, Oklahoma and other cities throughout America where blacks were wealthy and eventually run out by terrorist acts of white Americans against them. Black leaders don't talk about him and you know white leaders are not going to talk about him. The thing is this, why aren't black people aren't talking about him? They talk about the Million Man March in a whisper and it has been fifteen years now, well over a decade. And decades will come and people won't even know that two million black men and women assembled in Washington, DC because they don't want our children to talk about it now. They talk about the uprising in Egypt like there wasn't an uprising in Washington, DC. Okay, and look at what you see in Washington, DC today, the government basically took over when they pilfered and denied all kinds of rights from Congresswoman Eleanor Norton Holmes.

Our president gives us hope. We get pride and hope from our president because he's a black president in the

White House, that's pride. We are steadily looking for hope, what hope is, and what does hope really mean? Everyone else is getting something. Their sense of pride is coming from the fact that they worked for this country and got something for their labor. They feel hope because they can see that they got what they hoped they could get. We're caught up in symbolism that has no substance. You know, so no, I'm going to die in this and even if my own children don't follow me in social and political activism then they at least know what their daddy was fighting about. Now actually, my sons paid attention to the election to the point where they were studying and selecting aldermanic candidates and in turn telling their friends to vote for them. They would inform their friends and then tell them to go tell their parents vote for Alderman Austin- for example- and she won. I'm proud that even at the ages of thirteen and seventeen they were astute enough to tell their friends to make sure their parents come out and vote for an aldermanic candidate even if they didn't suggest the mayoral candidate. My sons followed the mayoral elections as well and when Chico lost said, "Dad we're sorry that Chico didn't win," but they know their daddy was involved in the campaign to make things better for them.

The next frontier for me is, like I said before, becoming a part of the speaking circuit. My agenda is the same as always but there is something dynamic about the impact that can be made from regularly scheduled speaking engagements to diverse audiences. I enjoy reaching out and connecting with people. I love speaking. I remember the first time that I spoke on stage in front of an audience. It was tripped out because once you get into it and you're speaking and you're realizing as you speak the shit that you went through, at the same time that you're speaking you're thanking God that you survived it.

It's an incredible feeling as you're walking across that stage or you're sitting down and you're speaking to the audience you say to yourself, 'I want them to leave here feeling one way or the other whether they like what I said or don't like what I said but don't dare say you didn't hear a damn thing of what I said.' You know, it's like you want them to take the positivity because when I speak I'm letting them know you can take it for what it's worth. I always tell them that you can Google me to find out more about me and what I'm saying.

Any person can look online and see that I have lived what I am speaking about; if you do something illegal, you're going to go to the penitentiary; I went there and I know. If you break the law you are going to the joint, no ifs ands or buts about it; you may get away but you're going to the penitentiary later because you're a law breaker.

There are consequences for the decisions that you make so don't think that you can do something and that the rules of cause and effect don't apply to you. When I speak to an audience I feel good; anyone would feel good, because you know if it is a ratio of 1 out of 100 and you changed their life and you saved their life you feel good because you feel like you have contributed to an individual becoming a better person. It's like a rush.

It is important to plan before presenting a speech. For example, when I know I'm going to speak for forty-five minutes I first ask the host or sponsor of the speaking engagement what their topic will be. Next, I ask them about the audience, like what type of audience to expect. If I am speaking to an audience of students who are attending alternative schools then I have to show them that they have an alternative and that alternative is to do right. If they are glorifying us as gang members and gang leaders I'm going to show them that this is where I went wrong and this is why we are doing these things to show them that they don't have to wrong. Furthermore, if they keep doing wrong 'the system' is going to make it where they will never have a productive life. So I tell them, I say, "Okay, go online so you can see who I am and then break me down into three categories: gangs, politics, and entrepreneurship." If there are nine students then I have maybe three of them take each one of those categories and let them go online. In essence they become investigative reporters. When I come in to speak- and after I have introduced myself- the facilitator allows the students to ask me questions; therefore, it becomes a participatory speaking engagement.

People have asked me on numerous occasions, how I manage to stay so energetic with all of my social and political obligations. They listen to me speak and wonder how I maintain my stamina for so many hours, especially at my age. I have to say that my energy and stamina come from healthy living habits. I'm a vegetarian who loves fish or I'm what they call a pescatarian. My diet helps me to keep my weight down. I practice safe sex and all that. My exercise is walking, dancing and having sex.

I enjoy serving my community and I am always busy. I have received some accolades during my career for the work I've done and I am a member of a few organizations. Jerry Butler brought me in to the Northstar Masonic Organization; I'm Masonic, 4 star number 1. I'm with a social group called the 'Rat Pack,' that's like the who's who in black business, politics, you call it. The first black Illinois Comptroller, Roland Burris was also member of the Rat Pack. I belong to NAN [Al Sharpton's National Action Network] and United in Peace. I am a member of the NAACP Economic Development Committee, the Target Hope Crime and Violence Committee, and the Coalition for the Remembrance of Elijah Muhammad. I've been recognized for my work by Mayor Daley of Chicago, Mayor James Maloof of Peoria, Illinois, Mayor Kurt L. Schmoke of Baltimore, Maryland and the South African Consul General Erica A. Broekhuysen. In 1989 the United Negro College Fund gave me the Fund Meritorious Service Award. I got the No Dope Express Foundation Outstanding and Dedicated Service Award in 1992; the God's Gifted Production Humanitarian Award in 1994; and in 1997 I was awarded the Center for Community Change Certificate of Achievement Award. And you know I get respect from the street organizations.

The anecdote from my life that would sum up who I am is... be god fearing; honor the women in your life; be a responsible parent in your life; and know, that you are an American not an African American. You are an American unless you were born in Africa and you came to America from the African continent. Your ancestors were Africans and so we identify as African Americans but we are Americans first. You may not always feel like an American while you're in America but when you travel abroad you will see how quickly you are classified as, American.

Understanding that you are an American means knowing that you have the same rights of any and all citizens of the United States.

12 OBAMA AND WEST

[A]nyone who looks beyond the glow of the moment will understand that neither we, nor our situation, will change overnight. A few of us have always succeeded, somehow, in spite of the failure of our American Dream. Barack Obama, through intelligence, will, self-determination, and yes, not a small confluence of favorable circumstances, may have reached his Promised Land, but most black Americans are still wandering in the wilderness…

The illusion of racial progress paves the way for a nationwide survival-of-the-fittest mentality. It will be okay to uproot urbanites so suburbanites can reclaim valuable metropolitan areas- gentrification is still unrelenting. Efforts to diversify the workplace and neighborhoods will become needless distractions. Affirmative action or any other race- or class-based efforts will become moot issues, of no value. After all, racism and prejudice died with the 2008 election. In a "post-racial" society, with New Media as its weapon, the brainwashing campaign now enters a phase that threatens to totally destroy our way of being... We've been programmed to deal with serious issues at a topical, epidermal level instead of going into deep tissue, to the root cause...

President Obama, utilizing a savvy new media campaign to change hearts and win minds (and votes), has opened the door for a counter-propaganda campaign- one that benefits not just black people but whites as well... We can seize this moment if only we take charge of our own destiny, our own reprogramming. If we pool our resources, we have the critical mass- the numbers, the voting power, and the persuasive skills- to enable us to combat the ills that derive from lingering racism. The same skills that have allowed us to survive, if used less passively and more pro-actively, can enable us to thrive.

Tom Burrell
Brainwashed: Challenging the Myth of Black Inferiority (2010)

Barack Obama is my favorite male politician today. I watched him, I know him. See it's different from everyone trying to make a connection and saying, 'Yeah you know he's a black man.' Nah, it's more than that, I really know him. I know the man and we could sit down and talk and signify. In 1996, when Barack Obama became an Illinois State Senator, he had become state senator by knocking Alice Palmer off the ballot and then he didn't have an opponent. She was the same individual who told him to get on the ballot in the first place. He saw that she didn't have enough petitions so he just knocked her off the ballot then became the state senator.

Soon after Barack had become an Illinois State Senator he said, "Man Gator, I'm going to run for the U.S. Senate," then he went and told Emil Jones, President of the Illinois Senate, "I'm going to run for the United States Senate." He told Emil that as president of the senate he had the power in his hands to assist his campaign efforts. At the time [Congressman] Bobby Rush was backing a white millionaire named, Blair Hull, for the U.S. Senate against Barack. The wealthy candidate whom Bobby Rush endorsed had spent somewhere around forty million dollars on his campaign. I remember one time Barack and I were sitting in a room together during the debates and a man had said something like Barack had fucked around with drugs and everything else. I looked at Barack and said, "Man shit, all you got to do is go out there and tell the truth." By the time he went on that panel-I think it was about 8 candidates- and he got finished speaking his truth, the next thing we know is all of those other candidates were chiming in and saying, "Yeah, I smoked a little refer; yeah, I did a little coke. I don't do it anymore." Yeah, yeah, when Barack came out of there I told him he was smiling. I told him, "See you done turned that panel into a Narcotics Anonymous seminar!" I remember we laughed hard about that. He won that race- with 70% of the vote- and became a member of the United States Senate in 2004.

Barack hadn't been a senator on Capitol Hill long before he went back to Emil; he said, "Emil, what do you think about me becoming a presidential candidate?" Emil asked him, "What can I do to help you?" Barack told him that he could help by saying that the junior senator of Illinois wants to run in the stead of Abraham Lincoln to become a president; Abraham Lincoln came from Illinois as well so that's how he played it up. Barack went out on the road with his platform and the Kennedys saw him out there. Ted Kennedy heard him speak at conventions and sent his daughter by private jet to meet with Barack to let him know that he had the support of the Kennedy family. The message she delivered was hey, we're going to have the money for you and we will make the network; with that- for lack of a better phrase- he was introduced to the Illuminati element, you follow what I'm saying. Barack was now dealing with a global power where he'd be around the people who make and dictate what happens everywhere in the world. He rolled with the Kennedys and became very close to them. The Kennedys brought that major political piece to the puzzle, that final link to his presidency. But hey, when you look at the road Barack Obama traveled that's why you hear him say, 'Hey, ain't nothing you can tell me about Emil Jones; he's my political godfather,' you follow what I'm saying.

As an American citizen I have a right to criticize Barack Obama because I have the right to criticize any president, you follow what I'm saying; it's an occupational hazard of being the president and a negro in America. Criticism or not Barack Obama is the greatest politician, male politician. I can say this and I know this because I saw him, I watched him and I knew him. Barack told me what he was going to do and he did it.

I have long admired the scholar and social activist, Dr. Cornel West. He has always been an iconic figure to me. Dr. West is our 21st Century Frederick Douglas even to the point of his attire and with the way he wears his hair. You can almost close your eyes and see the abolitionist within him. If you read any of his books you know he is about the end of modern day slavery like economic, mental and the prison industrial complex. Dr. West is a brilliant man, straight-forward, outspoken and unapologetically for the underdog. I first met Dr. West in the 90s when our gang summits were taking place all over the country to end the senseless killings and gang violence in our communities.

During those summits I also met the scholar Dr. Michael Eric Dyson who was active in the movement. Farrakhan was coming to all of our gang summits to speak then from that he started holding men's forums. The summits were the preemptive for the Million Man March. He made that call for the Million Man March one week from 'the Palace.' The Palace is his house in Hyde Park over on Greenwood Street, that's what they call it. I've been there several times. I met Spike Lee, Jim Brown and some more people there, at the Palace.

Dr. SaFiya asked me what I think about this supposed debate or alleged dissension going on between Dr. West and President Obama, my thoughts about the situation. I know how the media works and I think most of it is contrived to show disunity in the community and too many people are buying into it. When Dr. West and Tavis Smiley put together their Poverty Tour it was all about making sure that the poor were not ignored, they were giving them a voice. They were taking a stand for the disadvantaged and that's what I do every day, that's what Dr. King did, that's what Malcolm X did. Dr. West campaigned for President Obama, they were friends. Some people get angry and say that Cornel West is wrong for criticizing a black man or the first black president and we shouldn't be airing our dirty laundry and shit like that.

My position is that Dr. West is not criticizing a black man; he is making an objective observation about the president and the current administration. He is not criticizing the man he is looking at the position- the office of the president- and what is being done like he has with every other president. That is his right and my right and your right as citizens of the United States of America. West is a scholar and looks at the United States government with an analytical eye, that's what any socially and politically active person should do. He always stood for the people like he did with the gang summits. West isn't always fussing and even if he was, we all have some complaints and issues about jobs, schools, crime and some more.

The fact is, people are suffering and somebody needs to do something about it. Black and white; Latino and Asian; rich and poor; democrat and republican; West and Barack; all of us. When we stop being critical or objective because of race or political party- and everything else- that's when we stop progressing.

Dr. Michael Eric Dyson addressed the topic of criticism and President Obama in *Can't We Criticize What We Love?* (2011):

"I must disagree vehemently and stringently oppose the supposition that to criticize the President of the United States of America is to engage in bashing or hating... critics, those who have the best interest of the country at heart; those who respect the integrity and the brilliance of the president, as I do; those who respect his legitimacy as president should also be heard in our criticisms of his performance.

I happen to take issue with Mr. Obama on many things. Should I not say that? I love him. I supported him... Now that he is in office I reserve the right not only to love him but to criticize him. Like Toni Morrison said, 'Can't we criticize what we love?' I think the answer is in the affirmative... The job of a social critic and a cultural prophet... is to tell the truth to the best of his or her ability.

... After all, the president says to us we should be held accountable for our practices and behavior. We should hold him accountable for his practices and behavior as Chief Executive Officer of the United States of America and as the President of the United States. Black people must make up their minds to love this man but also to appreciate what his job is… also hold him accountable for our interests and plans.

Otherwise, when the next president comes- and most likely he or she will be white- they will say that you did not hold the black President of the United States of America accountable. Why hold anybody else accountable who is outside of your race?

We do not hold him accountable because of his race. We hold him accountable because of the office he occupies. Let's get that straight. We ain't hatin' if we criticize. We're not bashing if we hold him accountable. That is our job…"

13 HIGHEST REGARD

Respect commands itself and can neither be given nor withheld when it is due.

Eldridge Cleaver

Growth and Development for the Millennial Generation

I admire Harold Washington [The first African American Mayor of Chicago, 1983-1987] and he is undoubtedly chief amongst my favorite politicians. Harold dealt with the street organizations and I'm proud to say that I helped him to run for office. He was often under the attack and ridicule of racists in City Hall. One of my fond memories is the day Harold got in there and he told the three Eddies- Eddie Vrdolyak, Ed Kelley and Ed Burke- that he would come off that podium and beat their ass! We felt so energized because we had never seen a black man speak to power like he did. I had the privilege of meeting Harold Washington and working with him. As a matter of fact, he was the one who told Jerry Butler to run for Cook County Commissioner. My impression of Harold is that he stayed in the neighborhood, he walked around, and he was the Jack Johnson of black politics. You know Jack Johnson was that boxer [The first African American Heavyweight Champion, 1908-1915.]; well that's who Harold was. That's why he could say, 'you want Harold, here's Harold here I am,' you follow what I'm saying, he had cool swagger. You knew that he was HNIC, 'Head Nigga in Charge.'

When Harold Washington died from a heart attack a lot of people in the community said that 'they' killed him- referring to his racist opposition in City Hall. You want to know what I think about that? My thing is this, I believe Harold knew he had a weight problem and a health problem- you follow what I'm saying- and Harold could cook. I mean, he was a chef and when you're in power like that you don't allow everybody to cook your food. You have to cook your own food or have one trusted person in particular who prepares your meals. When you reach his level you're at the point where you take care of your own self now. I would never eat food prepared by random people if I was in that power like that. It's no secret, you know they do kill elected officials; they killed the Kennedys- you follow what I'm saying. You have someone prepare your food for you who you know so that's the least of your worries. You know, 'If I do die that'll be the person who killed me!' When Harold won that second term they knew he was going to be in a position to groom someone else to become mayor. So you know I hear people say that he had been poisoned and maybe he could have been; but, then again he knew he couldn't eat certain things, you follow what I'm saying. Harold was just as responsible for his death as anybody else saying that somebody else was responsible for him. You might figure that it is a good idea to hire your mother to cook. That ain't a question. Shiiiit, and hire somebody else in case she doesn't feel like cooking one day.

Carrie Austin, 34th Ward Alderman, definitely ranks among my favorite politicians today. When her husband, 34th Ward Alderman Lemuel Austin, died she ran for office and was elected alderman in the very same ward. Carrie Austin is my favorite because of all the things that she's doing out there in the 34th Ward. Any visitor to Chicago will see what I'm talking about. All up there on 119th they have a new shopping mall including major stores, restaurants and a gym; there was virtually nothing there before. The new mall has brought money and jobs to the community. Now they're building a complex known as the Salvation Army Village where they're going to have an Olympic sized pool, she's doing a lot of things out there. She didn't stop- you follow what I'm saying- she carried on that legacy. She's my favorite and the community shows strong support for her as well; even my children were out there campaigning to making sure that she won for re-election. Now she's over the budget committee, the most powerful committee in City Hall next to the Finance Committee.

United States Congresswoman Maxine Waters [California's 35th Congressional District] is a dynamic woman and also one of my favorite politicians. I hold her in high regard; she is a no-nonsense elected official. In 1998, when the Democratic National Convention was held here in Chicago she marched with us, the gangs to stop violence. She personally took me to Representative Conyers on the floor of the House Judiciary Committee in order for me to put pressure on politicians around the issue of police brutality and torture; specifically, because I was representing Aaron Patterson as his Urban Translator in his police brutality case against Jon Burge.

Anytime I want to get something done in Washington, DC I will go to Congresswoman Maxine Waters. She is a stand up woman and that's why when President Barack Obama wouldn't allow the Congressional Black Caucus an audience to help stop the violence I felt it was disingenuous. Later I found out that it was Rahm Emmanuel who was convincing him that he didn't have to deal with the Congressional Black Caucus. So it's like I say, this guy Rahm Emmanuel, he's a pistol. But one thing I can say about having someone there in DC like Maxine Waters… one thing I admire about black women- Dr. SaFiya included- you all have a way of claiming, saying and explaining some shit that makes a muthfucka do right. Okay, the first lady is right there to make sure that the president does right, as much right as he is allowed to do- you follow what I'm saying- and that's how I see Maxine Waters, making Congress do what they can do with the powers that she can do.

Among those politicians I hold in high regard, I must also include Representative John R. Conyers, Jr. [Michigan], Chicago's very own Representative Danny K. Davis and Representative Bob Scott [Robert Cortez Scott, Virginia]. They are all men who I know personally. I know I can count on them to take care of business in Washington, DC and they have my utmost respect. I have to include my respect for Hermene Hartman- who is not a politician- for her business savvy.

I admire Al Sharpton because he was a prodigy. I see the old tapes of him and remember when he was real fat and he was right there with James Brown; he even wanted his hair to be like James Brown, still to this day. I have a relationship with Al Sharpton to the point where we talk. Let me put it this way, I was in New York for his 2011 National Action Network Convention behind what we had done at his convention in 2010. Al Sharpton made mention of me for my efforts and results in the community. The 2011 convention is available on DVD and you'll see me there standing with Reverend Al Sharpton and Mark Allen. In his 2010 speech he urged people to go back to their hometowns and do things in particular- which he named- to better ourselves and the communities. Sharpton wanted us to assist him with making sure that the black farmers got their money. Well, the black farmers got their money; you follow what I'm saying. We were supposed to come back and get into voter registration and all that type of stuff here in Chicago to help with the political piece, right. Okay, well we did and check this out, Al Sharpton and my girl, Hermene are also working together politically. We were all together in New York that night. I keep NAN and Al Sharpton on my voicemail and that's why.

I met Al Sharpton in 1988. He was also there in 1994 on Capitol Hill to discuss the crime bill. At the same time Sharpton was planning to back Jesse, Jr. for Congress. Coincidently, there was a big scandal- involving child porn, bank fraud and sexual assault- going on around Mel Reynolds [Member of the U.S. House of Representatives from Illinois' 2nd district] and I said that he ought to be locked up. Well, Mel Reynolds was eventually locked up and Jesse Jr. ran for Congress, winning with five hundred votes from gang members. So, 1988 and 1994 that's how far back Al and I go.

I appreciate and respect Jesse Jackson for having the audacity and the fortitude to take me- who at the time was a gang enforcer- with him into the Oval Office to meet with Bill Clinton. He took me there to help stop a crime bill that proved to be detrimental to African American men and women. I knew Jesse in 1966 when he was the head of Operation Breadbasket in Chicago. That was right around the time Jesse was getting up with all the gangs. He was organizing boycotts in the city to get white business owners to hire blacks and use black contractors for services.

Beyond those days, I was collaborating with Jesse Jackson in 1983 when Harold Washington was elected mayor and in 1984 when he ran for president. Then in 1988 I was on Jesse's oversight committee for his campaign to run for president. I became a member of that committee because of my being down with Jerry Butler. I was traveling all over the country with Reverend Jackson as part of his oversight committee. It was during this time when I met Maxine Waters and all of them. I know all of them from way back. They witnessed my growth from a little starry-eyed young adult planning to see about liberation for Hoover and my development into a politically savvy man working to help elect a black president.

I admire my mother. I treasure both my mother and father because even though what they were going through things, they had respect for one another. Witnessing that relationship between my parents helped me to build my fortitude of an understanding of what love is.

I admire Larry Hoover for seeing the role I play in his

vision as an illustration; that I am an exhibit and the manifestation of what Growth and Development is all about. I admire him for using his power and influence to make sure that I couldn't get caught up in the game. Hoover did this by arranging things so that any individual who was to give me drugs for sale, even if I was paying to sell them, suffered repercussions. It was like I was an untouchable, 'Nah not him, nah he can't, he can't get in this game.' The word was, 'Let him be helpful in promotions and in other ways but he can't get in this game right here because we have to show that a person like us can evolve and progress.' Neither one of us knew that I was going to end up in the Oval Office or that I would make a move and get a pardon myself or any of that, you follow what I'm saying. We started off as a band of young stickup men but Larry knew the hustle that I had in me and the hustle that he had in himself- so he believed in me. Yes, I have a high regard for Larry Hoover. He sits at the top of my list with all the names of the people that I identified. I'm talking about these are individuals, outside of my mother and father, who are all a part of an equilibrium. No one is better than the other one; but Larry Hoover stands a step above them outside of my parents.

I have nothing but love, respect and admiration for my wife Terri and my sons; Leviticus, Kahdmiel and Waitari.

Waitari is my son who is playing international basketball over in Iran; he's a hero to me as well. He showed me that he's willing to go anywhere in the world to play basketball in order to provide a living for his family. He didn't get into the drug game, he graduated from Tulane College.

I am very proud of my daughter Africa who went on to get her master's degree after I stopped her from going to the penitentiary. I told her to reevaluate the people she was hanging with and the things they were doing like stealing fur coats and diamonds right out of jewelry stores. I even helped her into Narcotics Anonymous program. Now she has college degrees and is going around doing speaking engagements because she can show other young people how to change, how to evolve- from her own life experiences.

Africa's daughter, my ten year old granddaughter Alex, is my heart. She was able to see the difference between Carol and Pat Watkins at the DuSable debate and know for a fact that Pat Watkins could change her life around after being a crack addict because she knew how her mother had changed her life around. When my granddaughter went to school- she was telling me- how she told her girlfriends, you know her little friends, "Hey you all should have been there" Alex is so bright. When Rahm Emmanuel came to our church to speak she was telling her uncles, "Ah now watch, when he says this word he's going to put his hand this way. Watch, this is what he's going do," and he did exactly what she was saying. You know so it is what it is.

Wilson Frost is on my list of people who I admire. In 1967 he was the 34th Ward alderman and very much a part of what they called the 'Daley Machine.' Richard J. Daley appointed Frost as President Pro Tempore of the City Council for his dedicated service to the administration. Well, when Daley died according to the city charter Frost was supposed to automatically become mayor of Chicago. White officials in Chicago literally kept him out of the mayor's office by making the bogus claim that the keys couldn't be found. The city was very racist and there were a lot of individuals who talked about killing him so he decided not to assume his rightful place- by city charter- as mayor. They had somehow declared that the charter was wrong and appointed Michael Bilandic as mayor- Jane Byrne became the first female mayor of Chicago when she replaced him as mayor after there was a big snowstorm in the city. Then Frost was appointed head of the City Council's Finance Committee- replacing Vrdolyak. The Finance Committee is the most powerful committee in City Hall. Frost served on City Council until 1987 and didn't retire from service to the city until around 1998 from his position as Commissioner of the Cook County Board of Tax Appeals.

Musically speaking, I admire this young lady named Angela Charles; of course you know Jerry 'Iceman' Butler; my guy Curtis Mayfield; Marvin Gaye and Smokey Robinson. I also respect the political awareness of Hip Hop artists like Jay-Z, Kanye West, Common and Lupe Fiasco.

On November 30th and December 1st 2011 Jay-Z and Kanye West performed two concerts in Chicago at the United Center. I held a pre-concert press conference in front of the Michael Jordan statue outside of the United Center to support the use of their song *Murder to Excellence* as a call to stop the violence in urban areas. The lyrics from the song are powerful as they echo the voices of those who have been there and issues warning to others who needn't go there. My idea was that city-wide attention would be brought to the issue and the cause by having the song played several times throughout the day on Urban Radio stations like, WGCI, B96 and POWER 92. It was cold outside but the press conference had a good turn-out. Also, in attendance to speak in support of the *Murder to Excellence* Stop the Violence campaign were The Movement University's Jim Allen, Rev. Gregory Seal Livingston, Mark Allen, Judge Jesse Reyes, Judge Stanley

Hill, of course United in Peace and a wealth of other supporters from social, political, religious and community organizations. ["Hip-hop, the most powerful cultural force on the globe right now, was one of the ways in which the black underclass responded to being forgotten and overlooked, with its pain downplayed and ignored."- Dr. Cornel West, *Hope on a Tightrope: Words and Wisdom*, 2008.]

14 MS. IDA AND TERRI

The saint and the sinner are twin brothers... one was born but the moment before the other.

Kahlil Gibran

The Garden of the Prophet (1933)

The Autobiography of Wallace Gator Bradley, Urban Translator

My mother was a madam. Yes, madam, madam yes. That is right, they called her Ms. Ida. I'll put it this way; the hoes would come to my mom for her to arrange the date. The tricks would come to my mom for her to help pick the hoes. The trick and the hoes would leave their money with my mom. She orchestrated the whole ten yards. She was also in the drug trade and she ran the gambling. She was in the drug trade with Flukey Stokes, they were best friends. [Stokes gained national attention when he buried his son in a seven thousand dollar scaled down version of a Cadillac coffin.] She rolled with black gangsters, real black gangsters too like Nolan Mack [dubbed King of Dope and head of a multi-million dollar Cosa Nostra ring] and other high rollers. My mother, like I said, she was a madam and they called her Ms. Ida and I mean every hustler respected my mom, every hustler old and young. So, that's how I got pretty much into the game. It was like my DNA. My mother knew when I was locked up at the same time as my two brothers that it was part of the game. She understood you know if you do the crime, you have got to do the time.

My mother died right before I got the pardon. She died in 1989 and I got the pardon in 1990. She was the one who told me to get a pardon. My mother kept me in tuned to the streets out here to the point that I was sharp, you know, mentally and physically. My mother showed me, I'll put it this way... I'll never forget my father was doing construction, he was at work. I came home one day and there was another guy in the house- you follow what I'm saying- he was rushing to put his clothes on and get out. I was like, "Awww man this muthafucka up in here!" My mother leveled with me, she said, "Hey it's called making ends meet. Your daddy is the best man in my muthafuckin life," you follow what I'm saying. That's how I found out my mother was a madam she told me, "This is what I do and he knows this what I do and he's got his girlfriend and he do what he do but we make sure that y'all have what y'all got to have." I think I was thirteen then and that was my Bar Mitzvah, you know what I'm saying, if I were Jewish that's what it would have been. You know that's how they take their thirteen year olds and bring them into manhood, they give him a huge party to celebrate the age when he is considered morally and ethically responsible for his decisions, well that's what they do. For lack of a better phrase that was my Bar Mitzvah right there.

My wife, Terri, plays a major role in my career and my life. She is the ying and I am the yang. And sometimes she is the yang and I am the ying. [In Asian philosophy yin and yang are complementary opposites that interact within a greater whole, as part of a dynamic system. Yin and yang is used to describe how polar opposites or seemingly contrary forces are interconnected and interdependent in the natural world.] What I mean by that is…

My mother introduced me to my wife when I came back on the low end. Like I told you before, my mother was a madam and she was all off into the underworld as far as the Black underworld in Chicago. Anything having to do with the underworld, she was about it. So, when I came back on the set my mother was like, "Gator what you doin'?" This was in the 80s, it was about 1983 I think, between 1982 and 1983, and she was like, "Gator what you doin' back on this set?" I was just getting away from my first marriage and she said, "Gator you down here you either gonna end up in the penitentiary for the rest of your life or you're gonna be killed." My mother said this because she knew how hungry I was, you know. So, she called my wife Terri- well she wasn't my wife then of course- she called Terri and she asked, "Baby will you go get some cigarettes for me?" So, Terri got ready to go get the cigarettes and my mother looked at me and said, "Now that's somebody you're gonna need in your life." I was like, "Ma I ain't on that right about now. You know I'm tryin' to get back out here. I'm tryin' to get over love; you follow what I'm saying?" I was just going through coming out of a marriage- it was a good divorce- but I'm like mama knows I'm a sailor out here trying to see how I'm going to fit in and I don't know how deep I want to go back into this underworld shit. You follow what I'm saying. In other words, I was searching for what I could do with my life at this point.

When Terri came back from the store I told her- you know I'm high rollin' then- I'm like, "Hey you know you look real nice." I gave her five hundred dollars and I said, "Look, ain't no tellin' what Imma be doin' and you just a nice girl." She was working on LaSalle Street straight from Dunbar High School where they had a program sending young ladies and young guys to work downtown beyond the environment of the ghetto. So, Terri was working downtown at a bank and I'm thinking that the only thing downtown was the 'Magnificent Mile' because that's where I used to do my shopping, that's where I bought my flash. She showed me that LaSalle Street was the street that turned the lights off on Michigan Avenue- the Magnificent Mile- this is where all the power is; this is where City Hall is; this is where the county government is; this is where the state government is; this is where all the banks are; you follow what I'm saying. Okay, this is where all the law firms are and they make all the power deals right here. So, when I gave her the five hundred dollars and she threw the money on the ground and said, "I don't need this muthafuckin' money nigga, I'm workin. You know I'm not a hoe, I'm not that type of girl." I told her, "I don't think that you're a hoe. I'm just letting you know that I know what type of nigga I am." I went on to say, "I may be trying to duck up under your bed or store some shit at your house that you don't know nothin' about, your door gets kicked in, and at that point I don't care if you get arrested just as long as the weight don't fall on me." I told Terri, "I don't want you to be a part of that." My mother came and told her, "Girl, pick that nigga's money up. Take the nigga's money;" you follow what I'm saying, "don't throw the money down, take the nigga's money."

So, I'm high rollin' and working in that street environment. I also knew how to play, you know, dominoes and chess and all that; so when I went around the little white guys and the uppity niggas that were around them I'm playing their little games and they are fully aware of who I am because they are seeing it on the news. I had a nice pad; I had a mobile phone and a black Jag, you know so I was like I was the shit when I would go downtown to pick her up. I was always dressed to impress and they were like, "Who is this nigga here?! He goes to Hickey Freeman and has his coats cut." But Terri showed me that side of life and that made me smooth out my game and it was right in the same vision that Larry Hoover was talking about. I was like, 'Damn, ok,' and that's how I got political because I knew about LaSalle Street and the political power that was there.

When Jerry Butler was running for office I became his campaign manager. He was elected in 1986 and stayed on in the game. Then the presidential campaign was beginning right around the same time for Jesse Jackson, Sr. to run for president. I just mellowed right on in with that piece, naturally, and that's what Terri is to me. So, when we were going through our thing my humble was like, "You got a right to go anywhere you want to go and do what you want to do. My responsibility is to make sure that nobody hurts you while you're out there, you know, doing what you do. I got your back on that even when you aren't looking." When she comes back she knows the door is always open, so come on, you're free to go and I'm free to go but that's how we move, you know. Terri was like I say, she was the ying and yang that's why I understand and appreciate love.

15 PRAGMATISM

> Pragmatism asks its usual question. "Grant an idea or belief to be true," it says, "what concrete difference will its being true make in anyone's actual life? How will the truth be realized? What experiences will be different from those which would obtain if the belief were false? What, in short, is the truth's cash-value in experiential terms?
>
> William James
> *Pragmatism* (1907)

Loyalty is, key. Your word is very important and if, not if; but, when you find someone to love you've got to love them and not love at them.

Take life for what it is and that is, 'Ain't nothing guaranteed to nobody in life;' but, that doesn't mean you're going to stop living. It is important to seek knowledge and understand it- not that you've got to agree with it- thereby, you will appreciate wisdom, ok.

Understand that you have to make a plan and you have to work that plan in order to get something out of it.

Entrepreneurship is an ego without reservation or limitation when it comes to bettering yourself in order to be productive into this society. In other words, you've got to prove your worth to yourself in order to be productive in this society, you know. It's like this, for me to become an urban translator is entrepreneurship. I'm an entrepreneur with an entrepreneurial spirit. I created a profession and I became egotistical because no one could tell me what my pay scale should be for it, I made my own pay scale. Now, that's not having an ego where I'm stepping on somebody's toes. No, you just can't tell me what I should be paid. Why? Because I set the pay scale, you follow what I'm saying? You need to know that being an entrepreneur is just as important as trying to get a job to work for someone- being an individual. Once you're an entrepreneur you can create jobs.

I believe we have to share the same spirit of our grandparents and people who they knew who are now black success stories- entrepreneurs and hard working individuals. Consider Oprah's grandparents or parents, they had sixth grade or eighth grade or fourth grade educations. Now look at Oprah. Our grandparents, great-grandparents and some of our parents knew readin', 'ritin', and 'rithmetic, no spellin.' They were reading with an 'r,' writing with an 'r' and studying arithmetic with an 'r.' They weren't about spelling but they knew what the fuck they were doing.

I want to let young adults know that a gang is a group of individuals who meet sociably and regularly and don't let anybody tell them that it means anything different; it's not criminal. It is when individuals gather together to create a crime that they can be classified as a criminal gang. 'The Little Rascals' were a gang and you didn't see Alfalfa or Buckwheat being marched away in handcuffs at the end of every episode; they were a close knit bunch of young people- 'Our Gang.' You know and they need to know. I'm saying that to say, you can't pledge a fraternity or sorority and think that you're not in a gang. You can't become a police officer in the 'Fraternal Order of Police' and think you're not a gang. You can't become a member of Congress or a U.S. senator and think that you're not a gang. You can't become a member of the Democratic Party, Republican Party, or Tea Party and not be a member of a gang. You follow what I'm saying?

I'm just telling young people and I want them to see and I want them to get from this book that this is really not just another 'Keep Hope Alive' speech. I'm giving them and showing them how shit can happen and as it happened for me it can happen for them on the level that they set for themselves.

My message to the youth today is, 'Dare to Dream,' and fulfill your dreams to the point that you want in order to be a productive citizen to society. This is my message and my living legacy. Hoover once said, 'Real gangsters don't get old.' That's a legacy. Pushing the continuation of education regardless of what someone who is supposed to accrediting you determines to be your level or academic ability is also a legacy. I think if you can read, write and count that's very key to education because that's common sense. The life and legacy I hope to bequeath to African American men is that, hey even being an ex-felon I didn't stop, I didn't give up. I got my own pardon, I booked my own pardon. I created a profession as an Urban Translator and I can walk up into federal courts and I don't have to duck the federal government.

The legacy that Larry Hoover and I have established is to show individuals that you can belong to a gang and that's not criminal. A gang is only criminal when you create criminal activity, when you break the law. I believe there are so many legacies that I hope to leave. So, my legacy will be that everyone who stands up to make life and this world a better place for his neighbor is also showing his children that we all have to get along to live. I mean that is my legacy.

I thank God for Google. I thank God for the Internet. Thanks to Google and the Internet, even after I'm gone my legacy is going to be out there for anyone to see. I thank God for Dr. Hoskins, this is real. I thank God for Dr. Hoskins because she knows from whence I came- the Morgan Park community- and the struggle that her mother and father went through at quasi-integrated, racist schools on the Southside; the assassination of Dr. King and Malcolm X; Black Panther programs to benefit the community and so much more we experienced and things we did. We learned from our experiences and became activists- although her mother was always a militant sister; she was born a revolutionary- so that whatever they said about what we had to go through our children would have a right to a quality education. Our children have a right to education and whatever pits or holes they may fall into we have the right to tell them, 'Well dust your ass off and get your ass back out there!' We can say, 'You have the right to just do it because some of those white folk's daddies did shit far worse than what the fuck we did and their kids did far worse than what the fuck you did and yet they're still trying to run a corporation. So get on out there!'

16 CIVICS

We give you the facts. I told you information is power-knowledge is power. We can't be in an ideological battle to redeem the soul of this country if we don't have the facts.

Tavis Smiley

I believe in the value of Civics ["The study of rights and duties of citizenship… the study of government with attention to the role of citizens."] being taught in schools. I believe that just like the Jewish community, as a culture, teaches the [Jewish] holocaust to their children at home and in their schools; our culture should be taught that same way with that same fervor. I believe that our community would benefit by being educated this way because if an individual of another race can see what we went through to get to where we are now they'll have more respect and more love for one another. Even more, we would have more love and respect for ourselves and our community. That's why you're never going to see people in the Jewish community shooting and killing one another because they teach their children the importance of living, loving and respecting one another.

I also believe that the education of a child starts in the home. When parents share what they've been through and what they're going through with their children they can better illustrate for them what they are expected to do better. In this way, they can expect that they're children will do better. I earned my GED from a penitentiary. So, when I see my children graduating from eighth grade and graduating from high school and graduating from college that lets me know that they are doing better than me.

Although, I feel like I've got more common sense than them but that's the DNA in me.

My favorite books are *Message to the Black Man in America* [first published by the Nation of Islam in 1965]; *The Boss*, which is the story of the former Mayor Daley's father, Richard J. Daley [Mayor of Chicago from 1955-1976]; and, the book *From Gangster Disciples to Growth and Development*, which is the story of Larry Hoover's vision. ["My Alma mater was books, a good library... I could spend the rest of my life reading, just satisfying my curiosity."- Malcolm X]

The Message to the Black Man illustrates everything that Elijah Muhammad had been telling us we could achieve as people and then he demonstrated it. For those who didn't know about the concept of a 'Black Wall Street' [A term used to refer a prosperous black business district. More specifically, the 'Black Wall Street' in Tulsa, Oklahoma where in 1921 black businesses were annihilated and up to three thousand black men women and children were massacred by the hands of white mobs.] he made them aware because this knowledge helped [and inspired] black people to create black businesses. Elijah Muhammad showed- for lack of a better phrase- the glorification of segregation because it made sure we had our own black hotels, we had our own black stores. We had our own black businesses and it was segregated. We didn't lose everything until whites allowed us to integrate with them. Therefore we felt like, 'Well, I don't want to go the ma and pa store right there on the corner where Johnson is selling food now that they have allowed me to go into the white stores to buy food.' Hell, the food is more spoiled in the Arab stores than it was in the black stores.

Everyone needs to read *Message to the Black Man in America* because hear this, the white people are reading it; it's the black people who aren't reading the book. White people are reading the book so they know our message better than we do and they can manipulate that message when we don't know what it is supposed to be to begin with. They can change the meaning around and make it something different, we wouldn't know- how could we- if we don't read. It's like this, they want to rewrite *The Adventures of Huckleberry Finn* [by Mark Twain and published in the U.S. in 1885] and take the word 'nigger' out of it and try to put slave in place of the n-word. The black man in the story, Jim, had escaped slavery, he wasn't a slave he was free. He was a free man. So, they're trying to take the word nigger out of there and put slave in its' place when he wasn't a slave. He was a free man. That changes the meaning of the story. They're trying to do the same thing with *Uncle Tom's Cabin* [by Harriet Beecher Stowe,

1852] by taking out the word nigger. Some people argue that the n-word makes the story hard for 21st Century students to understand or embrace because they can't get past it. Other people say that if you remove the word nigger from the book then you are also taking away the context of the story. If you take the word 'nigger' out of *Uncle Tom's Cabin* then you are changing the story in a lot of ways. So all of a sudden they want to change, see just like they tricked us to bury the word nigger as if it has no significance to us. It does! You follow what I'm saying? A slave is a slave and a nigger is a nigger; however you want to play it. It can be 'that's my nigga,' or say 'that nigga crazy,' or 'I can't stand that nigga,' see that's three different meanings.

The book *Bos*' [Written by Mike Royko and first published in 1971.] talks about how the Irish in Bridgeport had a gang called 'the Hamburgs' [Richard J. Daley was elected president of the 'Hamburg Athletic Club' in 1924 and held this position for fifteen years.] and the way they went from being a gang to becoming a political force in this city and this country. Today they still have their clubhouse in Bridgeport. [From the year 1933 until 1976 Chicago's mayors were Irish-Americans who resided in Bridgeport (Edward J. Kelly, Martin H. Kennelly and Richard J. Daley); then again from 1989-2011 (Richard M.

Daley).] In *Boss* it shows where [Richard M.] Daley's father was involved in the Chicago Race Riot of 1919 which started when a little black boy was stoned and drowned to death because he accidentally drifted onto the white side of Lake Michigan. [The Chicago Race Riot of 1919 lasted for a week and ended with thirty-eight people dead; five hundred thirty seven injured and thousands left homeless due to destruction of their homes.] The book also talked about how the Daley's created a political organization that strategically helped Richard J. Daley to become the mayor of Chicago. Once in office, he picked his friends to be over different political organizations and for ranking positions from police superintendent to the fire commissioner to whatever it is; effectively creating a power. Not only did the power structure that Daley was a part of creating help to put himself and his friends in office; but, as proud Irish and faithful Catholics they were a vocal part of putting the first Catholic president in the White House.

Mayor Daley and his select group of friends helped to make Joe Kennedy's son president- and most of us know that Joe Kennedy was hooked up with the Mafia Family. You follow what I'm saying? Okay, I'm talking about with Lucky Luciano and all of them; he was a part of the mafia, he was just with the Irish Mafia. So, Mayor [Richard J.]

Daley and his crew hooked up Joseph Kennedy and the mob here in Chicago and together they helped John F. Kennedy to become the first Irish Catholic President of the United States. One of the things they did to help Kennedy win the presidency was to steal votes from the republicans. That's why when Gore was running for president [in 2000] Florida republicans basically told Bill Daley to get of town. See, the republicans in Florida told Gore straight up that their votes were going to Bush; so, Daley's brother Bill Daley went down there and tried to say it was wrong and they told him, 'get out this town we learned this game from your daddy.' That's how Bush became president, remember that? Stolen votes.

Boss is about a lot of things but one of the things that stands out in the book is how one ethnic group that had done all the wrong things evolved and ended up doing the right things in order to come into society and gain power. I would highly recommend for everybody to read that book. I tell my sons to read it- because I don't ask them I tell them- "read at least ten pages a day." My thirteen year old son is being told to read it now so that he'll know what they did and he'll know that he has the right to better his life too. And you know, to fast forward it, I want them to read *Boss* so that they can understand about how Rahm is coming into power with the help of Mayor Daley. I want them to see the connection and understand how Bill Daley ended up being sent to Washington to become Barack Obama's White House Chief of Staff after Rahm left from being chief of staff for Obama and came back to Chicago to become mayor of the city because Richard M. Daley stepped down from being the mayor. It's all connected and this connection has a history that goes way back, a long history that started with the Hamburgs.

The book *From Gangster Disciple to Growth and Development* shows how we used the book, *Boss*, to say that we have a right to better our lives; make our communities just as safe as their communities are; and, to tell our children that they have a right to do right as opposed to continuing to do wrong like their fathers. The Daley story could be called, 'From the Hamburgs to the White House' and ours is about standing for growth and development after our beginnings as Gangster Disciples. Everyone has the right to change their path or their station in life, for the better.

17 IMAGES

Forty-five years in the advertising industry have given me personal and professional insight into the power of propaganda- positive and negative- and the use of words and images to influence, change, and even transform people's lives... one of the greatest propaganda campaigns of all time was the masterful marketing of the myth of black inferiority to justify slavery with in a democracy...

The brainiac of his day, Thomas Jefferson- propagandist extraordinaire, chief strategist, and creative director, along with other powdered-wig power brokers- sold the idea of white supremacy to the masses- all the masses. They conspired to make this out-and-out barbarity America's first big brand. The early American ruling class used every available tool- religion, law, politics, art, literature, even the nascent field of science- as tools of their sales promotion and PR strategy.

The goal was to rationalize and reconcile the

development of a single society with two outrageously contradictory parts: one built on the concept of human freedom, the other built on vicious, governmentally sanctioned destruction of human freedom- all with the same history-making quill pen.

Tom Burrell
Brainwashed: Challenging the Myth of Black Inferiority (2010)

The images in the media of African American men that you see most everywhere you look are evidence that they don't want to show any black man who has survived. You follow what I'm saying? We are partially responsible for the images that we see because we are playing these roles as actors and buying into these portrayals as viewers and consumers. When you look at popular culture the 'powers that be' have continued to flood the media with negative images of black men. Part of this is the demand and part of this is trying to convince us that what we see is who we are.

Fortunately, there has been an emergence of African American writers, producers and directors in Hollywood who are creating positive images to be portrayed by strong black actors. These African American producers and actors are communicating from our hearts and our experiences. They care about the images that we have of ourselves. For example, when you look at Denzel Washington, a very distinguished actor, he knew he wanted an Oscar in the spirit that Sidney Portier, who is another very distinguished actor and trailblazer for positive black male images in Hollywood, received his Oscar. The Portier spirit or standard was, 'there are certain parts that I will play and certain parts that I absolutely will not play.' When you see Denzel Washington just close your eyes and you can almost visualize Sidney Portier where he's standing, it is because of that spirit. You see these two very distinguished and respectable men but out of all the powerful roles Denzel Washington played he got an Oscar for his violent role in the movie Training Day. Most people will argue that his portrayal of Malcolm X was an award winning performance. You follow what I'm saying? Okay, when you see the comedian, singer and actor Jamie Foxx, he just won an Oscar for portraying Ray Charles. In that role he's demonstrating that he is not a typecast actor. When you see a writer, producer and director like Spike Lee doing movies he is showing the black male image as a reflection of who he is. When you see someone like Ice Cube doing comedy films but still showing how black folks are surviving you are looking at us take control of our images. And when you see Tyler Perry who deals with serious issues and can still find a way to make the audience laugh, he shows strong black people surviving and black men in a positive light.

See we no longer have to leave it to the 'popular media' to show the image of a black man when their primary goal is to show that a black man can never and will never be anything- you follow what I'm saying. In the past we had to depend on the media to show us the images of ourselves; right now we don't have to depend on the media to show us the image of a black man all we have to do is look at the black man.

I never stop talking and reaching out to young adults. I am leading by example when I can tell them, "Hey, they can lock me up whenever they want to, they can create a crime and give it to me; but one thing is for sure, I can tell you that I haven't been back to the penitentiary for the crimes I committed over thirty years ago." I did not get a pardon from jail because I had a lawyer to negotiate a pardon for me. I went and got a pardon on my own by using the works that I had put into the community, my works and networks. I was a part of helping to elect the first black Cook County State's Attorney, Cecil Partee; I had worked extensively with Cook County Commissioner, Jerry Butler, who was over the Law Enforcement Committee; the State's Attorney came up under that, the sheriff came up under that, the public defenders came up under that- you follow what I'm saying- the county jail came up under that. Okay here it is, I once was a criminal and then my job was to go and investigate to make sure that the jails didn't have people still sleeping on the floors and fighting over what we would call 'dumpies,' you know the biscuits with the powdered sugar on it. So, when [Richard M.] Daley became the mayor of Chicago in 1989 it was up to the Cook County Commissioners to appoint the next states attorney; it was my job up under Commissioner Jerry Butler to go and do the polling. To make a long story short, Partee became the first black Cook County State's Attorney and the only black states attorney.

On the day I went before the Prison Review Board to get my pardon, the Assistant State's Attorney over gang crime tried to say- in so many words- 'Gator is not worthy of bettering his life; and so what he's working in county government and so what he hasn't been back in the penitentiary in the past fourteen years.' He went and told the Prison Review Board that he didn't feel that I should get his pardon. I asked the Review Board for a recess I made a telephone call to the Cook County State's Attorney, Partee. He sent me for the Assistant State's Attorney, I told that guy, "Your boss wants talk to you." His boss told him, "You go back in there and you rescind that objection because Wallace 'Gator' Bradley has proved that he's an upstanding citizen, as a matter of fact go back to your office I'm faxing you a letter of recommendation that Wallace Gator Bradley receive his pardon," that's how I got my pardon.

My life is an example of a positive black male image; a black man surviving and evolving and leading a purposeful life in spite of and because of the odds.

It feels very rewarding to hear young guys that come out the joint and say, "Hey man if it hadn't been for you I would still be in the penitentiary," or "I would've gone back to the penitentiary. And then you know my mother and father too." I'm like, you know, "Damn, okay I do, yeah."

For example, I went to a championship basketball game with my son Leviticus, the young one and one of his partners, named Josh. Sometimes Josh's father would take his son and my two sons to the game and then out for something to eat. They go out together oftentimes when I have to go to a political function or something- he's always right there. So, I had four tickets to sit on the floor at a championship Bulls game and I made sure that Josh was there with me because he and my son are real jammed. Alright, so I'm at the championship game and I hear a man shouting, "Josh you know you're supposed to do better than that!" I looked back and saw this man who looked familiar to me then I realized that I knew this man; come to find out it is Josh's grandfather. Josh's grandfather and I are the same age; we knew one another from the street and from being in the political arena, right. I told Josh's grandfather, "Man, I admire your son because your son makes sure that my son and your grandson are protected." At that moment I realized that I knew three generations of men and didn't know just how intertwined they were with me, and so they were sharing that same respect. So, that's the type of thing that happens oftentimes.

Sometimes it happens that I'm stopped by person who some people may consider to be a bum on the street. I always share with them because I ain't nothing but an argument away from being homeless my damn self, you know what I'm saying. But those very people are my little eyes on the street, they may hear something like, a nigga may walk past them and say, "Man we ought to get that nigga Gator." Well in that case my eyes on the street may find a way to get to me and to get the word to me before I turn that corner. They'll say something like, "Say Gator, say here, we know you ain't no punk or nothing but uh why don't you walk on the other side of the street and then go down that way because it's a nigga laying there waitin' for ya." I appreciate that because if it was the old me I'd be in danger or I'd have gone around the corner and got them first; but, they showed me how to get around the drama. When that happens- and it has happened- it makes individuals think, 'man how did he know about this shit?' Then they get worried, you follow what I'm saying. So, you know I'm humble with that.

I catch the 'El' sometimes. It's amazing that I can go to sleep on the El and a person can tell me if I caught the El for a whole week just to get downtown and that I got off on Jackson Street. I can catch the El and there may be a stop before Jackson when a guy might tap me on my shoulder and say, "Um Mr. Bradley, Gator, yeah hey man is this your stop coming up?" and I'm like, "Damn yeah dude thank you," you follow what I'm saying. That's because they're shocked to see me on the El, but they're watching out for me. So yeah, I'm real humbled by things that happen like that. A lot of times I receive kindness and consideration from total strangers. I take that as a blessing from God.

18 18-30 THEORY

The man who views the world at 50 the same as he did at 20 has wasted 30 years of his life.

Muhammad Ali

The youth today are much more intelligent than what the media or everyone else wants to portray them as. I'm sure young people are very intelligent, okay, and it's not that they're getting it so much from school. I think they're learning upon themselves. What I mean by that is our children grab new technology and run off with it, they pick it up quick and run fast with it. Just to show you how creative they are, with the use of blogs, Facebook, YouTube and an IPhone or other cellular phone they have a fully functioning movie studio and company. I mean with everything I named they can make a movie, broadcast a movie and talk about that movie all over the world! These young people didn't go to school to use all of this technology. That's very intelligent to me. In other words- for lack of a better phrase- that's just plain common sense for them in the 21st century, okay.

On the other hand, the shortcoming of too many youth today is that they allow the media to make them believe that no one can tell them anything. Unfortunately, too many of them buy into the narcissism and images of superiority dished out by the media to make them think they can make changes without listening to the wisdom of their elders, their parents or even gang leaders and former gang leaders telling them that there are consequences for the choices that they make.

The media puts it like they're a 'super-person.' What I mean by that is, they tell our children, 'Your parents are letting you down 'cause they really ain't tellin' you nothin' and yadda yadda yadda.' Even more, the youth are told that they really don't have to listen to their parents and if their parents discipline them they can call the police on them. In our day that shit wasn't even considered! You got your ass tore off when you didn't do what your parents told you to do! You see what I'm saying?! Okay, you damn ssshoooo... it was no backtalk to your parents. Today the kids feel like, 'you put your hands on me I'm dialing 911 on you.'

Okay, so the young adults are saying, 'we want a voice in this.' I'm going to put it like this for example, they're eighteen now and they come up with a proposed bill that says, 'We shouldn't be able to trust what anyone over thirty is saying.' It takes them five years to get it right so now they're twenty-three; okay, it takes them another five years to fine tune it. Now they're twenty-eight. When they finally get it implemented and passed they're twenty-nine. When everybody finally agrees and the damn thing becomes a law they're thirty. When they're thirty and think they can enjoy the law; but, they have forgotten that at eighteen they said that once you become thirty you shouldn't even be heard from.

The youth and young adults today have a wealth of potential. They proved this with the election of Barack Obama. They proved that when you look at someone like a Jay-Z who is about to become a billionaire, really already a billionaire when you put him together with his wife, you put both of their checks together. When you consider how he went from selling drugs to becoming a conglomerate- you follow what I'm saying- a business man, him and others, you see the potential that these young adult are living up to. When you see- and I'm just saying Jay-Z, there are so many others- or when you see Russell Simmons, who took the Hip-Hop industry and went way beyond an individual's means of potential. Or when you look at Will and Jada Smith who have conquered music and movies, now they are acting and producing for Broadway and Hollywood; and have started a school; and they have philanthropic organizations; and, they are raising their children to be successful creative artists. You follow what I'm saying. Like I said before, these young adults are intelligent and especially because of the way they can work technology.

We need to let them know that you set your own limits in life; but, you have to know that there is a limit to where you can go because you just can't go over that wall. I'm just being honest, being realistic. For example, you can't become president until 'the powers that be' say that they want to allow you to be president and when they allow you to be president- or to run for president- you have to cut deals that the average citizen does not understand. Why? Because then you're dealing with worldly events not local events, you follow me? And that's exactly what is happening with our president today and we need to understand that. When you've got the power in your hands to have a button pushed that will destroy an entire country then your conversation isn't the same as when you're hanging in the hood. You know what I mean?

Young adults need to know that there are some limitations, not necessarily self-imposed limitations. I'm talking about understanding this nation that we live in and how to play the game. Just like I know I could never run for office because they- the powers that be- know that if I become an elected official there are certain things I'm going to do because I know what to do with the money or the budget I would be given. So, my move is to help individuals become elected officials and to make sure that those who are elected do what they say they are going do. I stay in my lane. I know my limit.

The Autobiography of Wallace Gator Bradley, Urban Translator

19 KING DAVID

> Then David said to Nathan,
> "I have sinned against the Lord."
> Nathan replied, "The Lord has taken away your sin.
> You are not going to die."
> 2 Samuel 13-14
> *New International Version* of the Holy Bible

I know God guides my life because I pray just like King David prayed in the Bible. King David once saw a woman, Bathsheba, so beautiful that he could not resist making love to her even though he knew he could be stoned for committing the unspeakable crime of adultery. To make matters worse, she became pregnant with his child. King David sent for her husband, Uriah, to come home from war and tried to arrange for him to go home to his wife, Bathsheba, so that he could be fooled into thinking they conceived the child she already carried in her womb. Uriah considered it a dishonor to his fellow soldiers to take leave with his wife during a time of war and could not be convinced to go home. King David sent Uriah back to the battlefield with a note to his commander that it should be arranged for him to die. Basically, he put Bathsheba's man on the front line to be killed. When Uriah was killed King David married Bathsheba.

King David knew that everything he had done was a sin in the eyes of God. Among his punishments against the King, God cursed the son of King David and Bathsheba with sickness and death. King David started fasting and praying and asked God to forgive him for his sins. God forgave King David. King David was blessed with wisdom and a son with Bathsheba named Solomon who later became heir to the throne. My spirit was moved when I read the story of King David in the Bible. After reading the story of King David is when I knew that even though I may not be as pure as someone else and I may have sinned I can rest knowing that all we have to do is ask God for forgiveness. When we faithfully ask God to forgive us from the depths our hearts we will be forgiven because no one is perfect, we all make mistakes.

I went over to Israel and remarried my wife. We exchanged our wedding vows for the second time in Israel. We made love in the Sea of Galilee and conceived a child, my son, Leviticus. I bathed in the Jordan River where Jesus was baptized by John the Baptist. As I walked the sacred land, in Israel, with my wife I came to the realization that our soul- yours and mine- is at the bottom of our feet because as you walk that land you can feel the sanctity. You start crying because everything you read or heard about in the Bible is right there before your eyes, it is all around you and you can feel it.

You can see the Jordan River, the Sea of Galilee, and the Dead Sea. The Dead Sea has healing powers and people come from all around the world to take advantage of the Dead Sea's healing power. For example, you can wade in the Dead Sea with a case of athlete's foot but when you walk out your infection will be completely gone. You can lie on your back and float with ease because there are so many minerals in that water.

It's very simple to grasp why individuals can believe in miracles, they are all around you. When you visit that sacred place [Israel], anyone can understand why they are fighting over that land and why they will always be fighting over that land. It is so profound and hallowed that you can comprehend how they've been fighting thru biblical times even to this very day because of the power of that land; because no man can control that land, you follow what I'm saying.

You know and my thing is, when all else fails and you sit down and you talk to yourself; even when you feel you're at your lowest point; there is something that tells you to, 'just lay on down' and you know everything is going to be alright. At that point you don't know exactly what that means or understand how something is going to tell you 'just to lay on down' with so much weighing heavy on your mind but you somehow feel comforted and you lay your head on down. It is a peaceful feeling when finally you lay on down, you lay your burdens down and you rest your weary mind. When you wake up the next day you know everything is alright because you've been given another chance to try to make it all better. You have been given another chance. That's my spirituality. That is believing in God. You have to 'let go and let God.' I let

God handle all of my battles and whichever way he deems it, that's how I live it. I walk by faith.

I pray this book saves a lot of lives. I pray that others can learn from my journey and be enlightened. You need to know that you are never alone, someone has been there before and they know what you are going through; or, maybe they are going through the same thing now. Even when you are going through something and you don't tell anyone what you're going through talk to God and then listen for his response. He will always answer, whether it is a feeling, through a friend or maybe even a message in a book. I feel what many of the young adults in urban areas are going through because I've been there before and I am living proof that they can make it to the other side. Hey, don't give up, never give up.

Value your time and use it wisely. Your time is now, God has given you another day and you must get to work the same way he told Noah. Let me say it plainly; it went like, 'Noah, wake the fuck up! You're gonna build this ship.' Noah looked around like, 'Who you talkin' to, me?' 'Get your ass over there and build that ship!' You see what I'm saying? God gives us another chance and another day because we all have things that we are put on this earth to do. Each of us serves a purpose on this planet. Everything that we do will touch another life in some way.

Make it a positive way.

The Autobiography of Wallace Gator Bradley, Urban Translator

20 TRIBUTES

Most children have chosen action characters to be their heroes. My dad is my Superman, Batman, Iron Man, and Captain Kangaroo to say the least. His life has been a testament, from struggle to limitless possibilities. Every step of his journey, he has been engaged in the community. Even during his days of immaturity and desolation, he was always seeking ways to organize and redefine his path. Words cannot express the gratitude, love, appreciation, and happiness that I possess for dad sharing these past forty-two years of his journey with me and I tell you there was never a dull moment.

I was there eating breakfast with the Black Panthers, visiting the penitentiary, practicing with the El-Toros (a Morgan Park baseball league funded by my dad), shooting pool at the local pool hall with his childhood friends, attending Saturday EARLY morning service at Operation Push, assisting him with campaigning for himself and other candidates, etc. I could go on and on but the moral of this story is that he taught me that I have options.

When I was transitioning from a teenager to an adult, he told me, "Making mistakes don't define your story but it gives you focus and a desire to find your purpose on earth." Thanks to my dad's evolutionary process it enabled me, a teenage mother of two to go to Southern Illinois University, obtain three degrees, become a Social

Service Engineer, Doctoral Candidate, and advocate for disproportionate and underserved citizens/communities.

Today, with his guidance and leadership, I am a productive member of society, proud mother of three (Dewayne Hill, Porsche Bradley, and Alexandria Dillon) and Grandmother of Mekhi Bradley. United in Peace has molded my dad into a Hero, my hero.

Afrika Bradley, Daughter

My Father and Best Friend has helped me in more ways than you and I can even imagine. My father is a man of integrity, a man that has come from the bottom to the top, and when I say that I mean from the streets of War, Crime, etc. to a man who can help and save things that no other man or being can even imagine. I am saying all of this to express that I wouldn't trade my father for nothing in this world and my children are looking up to me to follow their Grandfather's footsteps and that is my plan.

I LOVE MY FATHER!!!

Thomas Watson, Son

The Autobiography of Wallace Gator Bradley, Urban Translator

Wallace "Gator" Bradley is the truth. Not the truth according to his perception, the plain truth. Gator has evolved and come of age. Not yet the best orator, but progressively better. His passion sometimes still gets the best of him, truth be told. What makes this book, his contribution, his story so relevant, is not only its consistency, but the consistency of him daring to change his life for the better so he can convince others of the necessity of change.

Hate his brothers, never. And those who desire him to do so don't serve a living God, so it's a mute point. He is distinctly hood and doesn't shy away from that fact. He loves his family, friends and of course, the hood. He is his brother's keeper and raises his offspring to give back the same. They are, like father, their own generation's brother's keeper. How then can one expect them to divide themselves from the people they grow up with, go to school with, make lifelong bonds and socialize with. Isn't that community? So if he lobbies for his brothers behind the wall to push the message to stop the killing, disrespect of elders and raping of women and children, don't expect they'll get a go home free card. It's about affording one the personal responsibility to make a positive difference right where they are.

Crime won't go away until the conditions that feed its

demands go away. But in the interim, why stand contrary to inclusion for the sake of improving humanity for all. Ain't that relevant truth?

Terri Marsh-Bradley, Wife

In the Most Illustrious and Holy Name of the One God of Unity, the Supreme Grand Architect and Father of the Universe.

It serves me no greater pleasure than to render a favorable testimony and introductory glimpse into the impact, the image, the voice and THE LIGHT of the Honorable Wallace "Gator" the Supreme Urban Translator, Bradley.

I AM Noble-Ameer Ali. The Hon. Gator Bradley is my adopted Father, Mentor, and Benchmark for moral and cultural excellence. He is affectionately and in essence "My YODA" and one of the last living legends of the Grassroots JEDI. For over 20 years, I have sat under his tutelage at United In Peace, Inc.

In order to grasp a modicum of understanding the depth and breadth of Mr. Bradley, one would have to understand one of the many facets of this Master's Diamond Cut in America's rough. Mr. Bradley is the Co-founder and current President, Secretary and Sovereign Grand Commander of United In Peace, Inc. This organization and movement among many other successful initiatives spawned from his vision and the shared vision of the Hon. Larry Hoover primary Founder of United In Peace, Inc. has become the next generation of innovative solutions to the violence plaguing urban America and also an effective and efficient solution to the social ills of our communities.

Mr. Bradley has personally empowered me with the motto, "the power to change through public safety, education and the willingness to live united in peace as a way of life."

Under his mentoring and the Love of a Father that I was never awarded as an at-risk youth, I am happy to say that I have sacrificed and dedicated my life to the good fight in community and social service for the sake of our children's salvation.

In the Vision of the Hon. Larry Hoover and under the guidance of the Hon. Gator Bradley and several other grass roots leaders and civil / human rights freedom fighters… I have been able to transmute my life from the unwholesome darkness of ignorance and arrested development to the marvelous light of public servant and lifetime friend of humanity.

My path in the way of life and philosophy called Growth and Development has taken me on a beautiful journey to master the many philosophic paths of light, from far eastern homeopathic sciences and medicines to the western mother of mysteries found in the halls of Egyptian Freemasonry. The Honorable Larry Hoover and Gator Bradley inspired and mandated in me the pride and extraordinary accomplishment of education prowess and business acumen in preparation for excelling in corporate America and my global outreach to uplift fallen humanity.

I have gone from lying at the horizontal level of a shallow grave as an ex-gangbanger and detriment to society in my juvenile delinquency and upon hearing the call to excellence by the voice of the true teachings and vision of the Hon. Larry Hoover and my Father Gator Bradley… I have been blessed in alignment with the will of God to achieve such success in the private and professional sector including but not limited to:

-Tennessee State University, Computer Science and Software Engineering

-Legislative Assistant and Intern to the 100th General Assembly of the Tennessee State House of Reps.

-Website design and social media technologist

-Six Sigma Black Belt

-ISO 9001:2008/ TS:16949:2002 Lead Auditor Process Control and Improvement Engineer

-Risk Management and Safety & Environmental Specialist

-Public Safety Consultant

-Youth Intervention Counselor

Etc. Etc. Etc.

These few accomplishments in this mortal life gives me reason to always pause and remain humbly grateful that I had the blessing to have these great leaders and this great philosophic discipline of the concept of (GROWTH AND DEVELOPMENT) in my life to intervene and turn my path from self destruction and cyclic recidivism to the light of being a positive asset to American society and the key to uplifting our at-risk youth and global community at large.

Today, I am blessed to serve as the Executive Director and Co-Chairman of United In Peace, Inc. To get the total impact of our reach, depth and breadth… you can witness our innovative model of real-time online intervention and read the many cross-demographic testimonials in support of our missionary work to reach teach and save our at-risk communities of Urban America. Our impact and outreach allows us to discover and input preventive controls to the root cause of the social ills and the systemic findings suffered by so many children throughout America.

Our problems and our solutions offered to our problems as an antidote cuts across all ethnic, social and economic divides of life and actually has a positive and healing impact upon the entire human family. United In Peace, Inc. as a result of our social media ministry and online intervention campaigns has allowed us to be visible and heard by well over 23 countries thus far. For more light… please visit our corporate fan page on Facebook at your convenience.

www.facebook.com/unitedinpeaceinc

TO GOD BE THE GLORY for allowing me to be one of many humble examples of the Good that we as Urban America can produce through brightening the hopes of our Youth and letting America know the truth about the Vision of the Hon. Larry Hoover and my Father Wallace Gator Bradley.

UNITED IN PEACE YESTERDAY, UNITED IN PEACE TODAY AND UNITED IN PEACE TOMORROW. AS WE PEER OVER THE GLORIOUS HORIZON OF THE NEXT MORNING TO OUR STRUGGLE FOR CIVIL AND HUMAN RIGHTS WE GIVE GOD THE GLORY AND WE ARE ASSURED THE COMFORT OF KNOWING THAT THE RESURRECTION IS A FACT AND WE SHALL SEE OUR GREAT ALCHEMICAL WORK TODAY IMPACT THE ENTIRE WORLD WHEN NEW MORNING COMES AS A GLOBAL SOCIETY BEING MOVED A LITTLE CLOSER TO BEING UNITED IN PEACE.

I remain your Humble Servant, Friend and Brother in Our Universal Struggle to Uplift the Human Family.

NOBLE-AMEER ALI, EXECUTIVE DIRECTOR & CO-CHAIRMAN,
UNITED IN PEACE, INC.

www.unitedinpeaceinc.org

unitedinpeaceinc@gmail.com

SERVING 1993 -2013 AND BEYOND

UHURU NA UMOJA "FOR FREEDOM & UNITY"

I depart as I came in Peace and Love for Humanity and Illuminating Hope for Our Future.

****

Please take some time to know who we are, what we are dedicated to and what we as a people want.

United In Peace, Inc. is a lawfully incorporated non-profit 501.C.3 private foundation / movement in the Great State of Illinois since 1994 being established in late 1992-1993. We are totally dependent on our donors and sponsors like you to further our process improvement, programming deployment and evolutionary impact on changing the lives of several thousand children across America who need immediate intervention or character adjustment from positive mentors to save our young men and women from the clutches of violence, drugs, gang activity, recidivism of incarceration and the unwholesome darkness of illiteracy and malnourished education. Won't you help us to restore our children and young adults at-risk back into the marvelous light of legitimate upstanding and productive members of American Society?

FREEING, UNITING AND ACCEPTING... Men and women of all tribes and grassroots movements, (ALL) races, nationalities and walks of life who demonstrate legitimate upright conduct and acknowledge a belief in God, United In Peace, Inc. and its sacred arts, crafts and methodologies of intervention and outreach, is a private and charitable foundation, deriving its powers from the heart of God and the inalienable human and constitutional rights guaranteed to all citizens of our Most Illustrious United States of America. Thus We the Sons and Daughters of United In Peace, Inc. remain faithful to these edicts and divine principles of civilization, inculcating harmony, fellowship and brotherly & sisterly love among its members.

(((ENLIGHTENMENT & ILLUMINATION)))

UNITED IN PEACE, INC. shall establish and set aside lawful and duly CHARTERED & STYLED CONCLAVES OF PEACE AND MORE LIGHT to provide enlightenment through ancient and modern symbols, allegorical lessons, and education endeavoring to strengthen and improve the character of the individual man and woman; enhancing his or her moral and spiritual outlook, so he or she may adapt a life exemplifying the principles of personal responsibility and righteous living and in all righteous endeavors.

(((BENEVOLENCE)))

Thus, THE SONS & DAUGHTERS OF UNITED IN PEACE, INC. as WE STRIVE IN (OUR STRUGGLE) to promote community and human welfare and inspire acts promoting benevolence, charity and good will toward all mankind; translating OUR SACRED principles and conviction into personal actions ultimately making the world in which they live a better place and a little closer to being UNITED IN PEACE!!!

SO MOTE IT BE!!! AMEN AMEN AMEN!!!

United In Peace, Inc. is happy to announce that in 2013, we are enjoying our 20th anniversary of its great missionary work for the direct and indirect intervention and mentoring of our at-risk children and inner city urban citizens throughout the country.

While the initiatives of United In Peace, Inc. have grown and developed exponentially, we have remained a consistent beacon of light in serving our primary objective of putting a stop to the gang-banging, bullying, cyber-bullying, violence, senseless shootings, rape of our women and the disrespect and robbery of our elders and senior citizens throughout our illustrious country.

God Bless You and May God Continue To Bless The United States Of America... the Country, GRAND EXPERIMENT & Global Gift that was MASTERFULLY BUILT and Given to the WORLD By OUR Ancestors!!!

THE SCIENTIFIC AND PHILOSOPHIC SOCIETY OF (GROWTH & DEVELOPMENT) AND ITS MODERN MOVEMENT FOR SOCIAL JUSTICE AND THE SECURITY AND ADVANCEMENT OF CIVIL AND HUMAN RIGHTS.

THE CAGED TIGER OF GROWTH & DEVELOPMENT...

THE CAGED TIGER OF GROWTH AND DEVELOPMENT FOR THE POOR PEOPLE OF URBAN AMERICA AND THE ENTIRE WORLD...

(((WILL NOT BE BOUND AND WILL NOT BE HELD ANY LONGER!!!)))

WHAT DO WE WANT?

WE AT UNITED IN PEACE, INC. WANT FREEDOM TO BE UNITED IN PEACE AND TO STAY UNITED IN PEACE WITH OUR BROTHERS AND SISTERS HERE THERE AND EVERYWHERE DISPERSED THROUGHOUT THE GLOBE...

STANDING IN SOLIDARITY WITH ALL NATIONS, TRIBES, GRASSROOTS MOVEMENTS AND STREET ORGANIZATIONS WHO ARE HONESTLY DEDICATED TO UPLIFTING THE COMMUNITY AND WHO CAN STAND THE PRESSURE OF FIGHTING THE GOOD FIGHT FOR THE SALVATION OF OUR CHILDREN AND FUTURE.

WE WANT THE FREEDOM TO EVOLVE FROM GANGSTER DISCIPLES TO GROWTH AND DEVELOPMENT, AN ASSET TO OUR COMMUNITY AND A SOLUTION TO OUR COUNTRY'S SOCIAL ILLS, WITHOUT BEING CAGED, HEDGED AND TOLD BY THE CORRUPT SYSTEM THAT YOU CANNOT BE ANYTHING ELSE BUT GANGBANGERS. WE WANT THE TRUTH TO BE KNOWN ABOUT OUR STRUGGLE TO BECOME A PART AND PARTIAL OF

LEGITIMATE AND UPSTANDING AMERICAN SOCIETY.

WE WANT THE FREEDOM OF UNITY WITHOUT THE CONCERN OR INTERFERENCE OF RENEGADES, DISSENTERS, AGITATORS, AGENT PROVOCATEURS, PROPAGANDIST, FRAMERS AND THE SCIENTIST OF YELLOW JOURNALISM!!!

WE WANT FREEDOM FROM POVERTY AND PHYSICAL, MENTAL & MORAL SLAVE LABOR!!!

BOYCOTT THE DAMN SWEATSHOPS TILL THEY SWEAT JUSTICE AND FAIR WAGES!!!

WE WANT FREEDOM TO PURSUE LEGITIMATE HAPPINESS & PROSPERITY WITHOUT OPPRESSION OR THE FEAR OF MUNICIPAL BRUTALITY OR RACIAL PROFILING!!!

WE WANT FREEDOM OF OUR CHILDREN'S PRE-MATURE DEATH BY SELF-IMPOSED WAR & VIOLENCE FROM THE WORLD WITHIN GHETTO AMERICA AND ALSO THE EXTERNAL WAR AND

VIOLENCE BEING WAGED AND INFLICTED UPON OUR CHILDREN COMING FROM THE WORLD OUTSIDE OF URBAN AND GHETTO AMERICA!!! WE SAY ENOUGH IS ENOUGH TO THIS INTERNAL AND EXTERNAL WAR!!!

WE WANT THE FREEDOM TO TEACH REACH AND CHANGE OUR AT-RISK CHILDREN'S LIVES FROM NEGATIVE TO POSITIVE, FROM CORRUPT TO LEGITIMATE, FROM ILLITERATE TO LITERATE, FROM IGNORANT TO INTELLIGENT, FROM DETRIMENT TO ASSET, FROM THE SHALLOW AND HORIZONTAL GRAVE TO PERPENDICULAR AND VERTICAL SUCCESS IN THE MARVELOUS LIGHT OF SOCIETY WITHOUT THE FEAR OR REALITY OF BEING SABOTAGED BY DARK FORCES AND PRINCIPALITIES OF HIGH PLACES THAT (PRAY) AND (PREY) FOR OUR DESTRUCTION!!!

WE WANT THE FREEDOM OF ALL OUR POLITICAL PRISONERS BEING HELD FOR POTENTIAL POLITICAL INFLUENCE TO EFFECT THE NEEDED CHANGE IN THE SYSTEM AND CHANGE FOR THE BETTER IN THE

COMMUNITY!!!

WE WANT THE FREEDOM TO FIGHT FOR FREEDOM WITHOUT FEAR OF THREAT OR RECOURSE!!!

WE WANT EMPLOYMENT ON PAR WITH A FAIR AND HUMANE PAY-SCALE…AND THE FREEDOM FROM BEING DRIVEN BY THE BULLWHIP OF SLAVE LABOR AND THE TOIL OF RUNNING THE RAT-RACE TRYING TO MAKE IT FROM CHECK TO CHECK!!!

WE WANT JOBS BUT MORE SO WE WANT THE ABILITY AND FREEDOM TO CREATE AND PROVIDE LEGITIMATE JOBS FOR OURSELVES!!!

WE WANT THE FREEDOM OF (((EDUCATION))) WITHOUT BEING BANISHED TO A LIFETIME OF CREDIT PENALTY AND IRS OPPRESSION MAKING US SLAVES TO STUDENT LOANS!!!

WE WANT PEACE BETWEEN ALL TRIBES, NATIONS AND MOVEMENTS OF URBAN

AMERICA GIVING BIRTH TO GLOBAL PEACE AND THE FREEDOM FROM VIOLENCE WHERE OUR CHILDREN MAY HAVE PEACE AND ENJOY THE SAME OPPORTUNITY OF SURVIVAL AND PROSPERITY THAT THE ULTRA RICH ENJOY!!!

THE AFFLUENT AND ULTRA RICH INTERNATIONAL NETWORK OF GANG-(BANK)STERS AND THE MEGA-WEALTHY CORRUPTED OFFICIALS OF THE WORLD, WILL ONE DAY SOON TAKE SO MUCH FOOD OUT OF THE MOUTHS OF THE POOR PEOPLE OF THE WORLD…THAT ONE DAY SOON….THE POOR PEOPLE OF THE WORLD WILL HAVE NOTHING LEFT TO EAT OR FEED UPON BUT THE RICH!!!....WE THE POOR PEOPLE OF THE WORLD WANT SOLUTIONS TO OUR STARVATION INSTEAD OF BEING FORCED TO HUNT, PREY AND FEED UPON THE CORRUPT RULERS AND THE MEGA WEALTHY SWEATSHOP SLAVE-DRIVERS OF THE HUMAN FAMILY!!!

WE THANK GOD FOR THE SPIRIT, HEART AND SOUL OF PHILANTHROPY AND THE WEALTHY FREEDOM FIGHTERS WITH PURE HEARTS THAT GIVE BACK TO THE

COMMUNITY...THIS IS THE ONLY THING SAVING THIS WORLD AS WE KNOW IT!!!

WE WANT THE FREEDOM TO LOVE, PROTECT & DEFEND OUR COUNTRY, THE UNITED STATES OF AMERICA AND TO HAVE OUR COUNTRY LOVE US BACK WITHOUT BEING TYPECAST "THE NEGRO PROBLEM" OR PROFILED AS A CANCER AND LIABILITY ON EARTH!!!

THIS IS THE PRAYER THAT WE DELIVER TO THE FOOTSTOOL OF THE HIGH AND ROYAL THRONE OF THE MOST HIGH FATHER/MOTHER GOD OF CREATION IN THE HIGHEST COURTS OF HEAVEN!!!!

CONSIDER IF YOU WILL A QUESTION TO MEDITATE UPON MY BEAUTIFUL BROTHERS AND SISTERS OF OUR STRUGGLE FOR PERFECTED & BETTER GROWTH AND DEVELOPMENT...

THE WISE MASTERS OF THE ANCIENT WORLD ASKED THE QUESTION:

(((WHAT TRULY CAGES THE TIGER? IS IT THE BARS OR IS IT THE SPACE BETWEEN THE BARS???)))

THE PHYSICAL IS AN EASY DOMAIN TO CONQUER; THE MENTAL, MORAL & SPIRITUAL SOUL-PLANE IS THE TRUE BATTLEFIELD FOR (GREAT) MASTER-MINDS!!!

THE HON. LARRY HOOVER ONCE SAID...

"It is a fact, without contradiction that the success of any movement depends largely upon the participation of the mass of people involved in that particular struggle. Our New Concept teaches that our organization is based on GROWTH & DEVELOPMENT. GROWTH & DEVELOPMENT builds in stages and degrees. It is not cool and romantic; it is stalking and being stalked; it is (((THE SYSTEM))) rising above our level of intelligence to repress us; and it is our membership learning how to counter their repression and again pull ourselves above their efforts to destroy us."

UNITED IN PEACE, INC. SAYS TO GOD BE THE GLORY FOR SENDING US THE KEYS TO FREE THE CAGED TIGER OF GROWTH AND DEVELOPMENT FOR ALL POOR PEOPLE OF THE ENTIRE EARTH!!! AMEN AMEN AMEN…SO MOTE IT BE!!!

1. The Book of Revelation Chapter 20 verses…

4) And I saw thrones, and they sat on them, and judgment was committed to them. Then I saw the souls of those who had been beheaded for their witness to Jesus and for the word of God, who had not worshiped the beast or his image, and had not received his mark on their foreheads or on their hands. And they lived and reigned with Christ for a thousand years.

5) But the rest of the dead did not live again until the thousand years were finished. This is the first resurrection.

6) Blessed and holy is he who has part in the (first) resurrection. Over such the second death has no power, but they shall be priests of God and of Christ, and shall reign with Him a thousand years.

TO GOD BE THE GLORY FOR THE SUNRISE OF THE 2nd RESURRECTION OF UNITED IN PEACE INC.

TO GOD BE THE GLORY FOR THE 1st, 2nd AND NOW THE DAWN OF THE 3rd RESURRECTION OF GROWTH AND DEVELOPMENT FOR URBAN AMERICA AND THE ENTIRE URBAN WORLD!!!

MAY OUR SPREAD-EAGLED WINGS OF KNOWLEDGE, WISDOM AND UNDERSTANDING FLY WITH YOU FROM THE HORIZONTAL BASE OF (360°) TO THE VERTICAL UPPER LIMITS OF (720°) AND BEYOND BOUNDARIES WITHOUT MEASURE!!!

Noble-Ameer Ali, The Comforter & Conqueror

True Leadership Passing The Torch
(Bridging The Generation Gap)

Introduction

My name is Orlando Henry; in the streets I'm called Lando Magic. I am an Urban Translator for United in Peace and the former Research Team Developer for One Family One Community, a non-profit organization based in Minnesota. Previously, I co-hosted two talk shows on BlogTalkRadio called *Awareness 2 Conscious Minds* hosted by myself & Maleta Kimmons (a mutual & dear friend of Gator & myself, we all call her Queen Nuchie) and *BORN GOD MADE GANGSTA* hosted by Bro. Eric X & myself. I was a partner in Alabama Hott Radio.com (as an on-air personality for *The Smokin' Session w/ DJ Kristylez & Chillin' @ Da Trap w/ DJ Firestarta*.) I am currently Management Consultant for DJ Firestarta, Co-owner and Founder of Flame On Radio (www.flameonradio.com) which was founded by DJ Firestarta and myself. I'm also a partner in a music production company called Breakin' Bonez Productions with a Brother by the name of Paul Hesser aka Paule Bonez. I'm also a music & talent promoter when I'm not performin' or entertain' myself, as well as a self-employed Tattoo Artist. I'd like to say "I'm a jack of all trades & master of some...lol." I was born &

raised in Birmingham, AL. I've work alongside with Gator Bradley goin' on 5yrs.

My Early Influences & Reading About AND Watching The Man Before I Got To Meet The Man (The Beginning of The Torch Passing)

I first started readin' up on Gator back in 1992 at the age of 11 through the *Final Call* newspapers that my oldest brother La'Vincent Henry used to bring home. He was the first in our family to be a part of The Nation of Islam & Growth & Development. We was raised Baptist so him becomin' a Muslim was a slight problem due to the ignorance of not learnin' of the culture from my family. At first I was somewhat ignorant until my brother explained "We Worship God too, we jus' call him Allah." When he broke it down to me like that I understood & shed my ignorance of that subject. My brother knew I liked to read aside from the fact he caught me readin' his papers (*Final Call*) so whenever he finished the ones he read then I'd read 'em. One time I read *Final Call* and it was talkin' about the Gang Summits of 1992 & it mentioned Gator & Spike Moss (who I've also had the pleasure to work with.) My brother would always say "that Brotha Gator Bradley da truth." I never thought in my life that would I be workin' alongside these folks but time showed me otherwise.

As time passed, by the time I turned 13yrs old I slacked up on readin' & started interactin' wit' tha street life. I started hangin' wit' Gangster Disciples in my neighborhood & started gettin' into all kinda bullshit, foolishness, & more foolishness. I didn't become a member until I was 15-16 yrs old. I had been heard about the new concept of Growth & Development by that age but them guys here at that time wasn't on that or tryin' to put us on that at the time. But it would always raise a question in my mind why not if 'The Old Man' (Larry Hoover Sr.) was on the Geto Boys album *The Resurrection* sayin' this is what We suppose to be on not to mention publishin' the book *FROM GANGSTER DISCIPLE TO THE BLUEPRINT: GROWTH & DEVELOPMENT*!

At the age of 17, my oldest brother introduced me to a Brother from Chicago who was workin' with him at Mazers Funiture Company who put us both on point & from that point on I been strivin' to live the concept of Growth & Development.

I remember back in the days when cable TV was higher than heroin addicts on the weekend. I would watch Chanel 9 News in Chicago & they would show Gator runnin' for Alderman. No matter how they would try to tear 'em down and throw up his past he still would not budge or stop. It put me in the mind of a devoted civil rights worker from way back. Me bein' from Birmingham steeped in the Civil Rights Movement it made me start thinkin' one day that can be me! I've always had a thang for The Black Panthers & the Civil Rights Movement as a child; I always wished I was around in those days & times hell Gator was there!

What really truly started openin' my eyes to make that change & live fully by Growth & Development was when my oldest brother/ father figure went into the Federal Prison System in 2002. He would stay on me about comin' out the streets & started sendin' me the proper readin' material; one was a magazine article by DON DIVA Magazine which interviewed Gator about 'The Old Man' (Larry Hoover Sr.) which set in my mind, "one day I'mma get up wit' Gator one of these days." Then I look again, in 2007, I'm watchin' American Gangster & who they talkin' about but 'The Old Man' (Larry Hoover Sr.) & Gator is on there once again keepin' the message goin' strong as always. So, it set in my mind without a doubt "I gotta get up wit' Gator Bradley."

With time comes patience, so I started gettin' hip to the internet around 2005-2006; but, I didn't start Facebookin' until 2008. It wasn't until late 2008 or early 2009 that I found Gator on Facebook through a Brother named

Rasheem Glover out of New York; if not for him I'd never came across Gator. Once properly introduced to each other we hit it off immediately. I remember one time this dude called himself "cyber beefin'" talkin' ignorant to Gator & Bro. Rasheem being real Disrespectful about the Growth & Development movement. So, I asked Gator "you want me to get up wit' dat jokah & see were his head at?" Gator was like, "Somebody need to see what that dude on." So, Rasheem & myself got up with that fella... I tell you this, Gator was right. Dude ain't have the common sense God gave a fruit fly! So, I asked Gator, "How you want me to go about exposin' this foolishness?" He said "Shhhheeeiiit... Do what you do fam." I said to myself, "why you tell me that fo'?" Man we roasted that joker for 74 hours 'til some of the family called Gator to call me off of 'em. Gator told me to call 'em so I did and the first thing he said to me was, "Mane y'all gave that fella the business... Mane you funny as hell, you had my side splittin' but gone stop it because you don't want nobody to say you're cyber bullyin' even if it is jokes." That's what started the foundation of him mentoring me & the beginin' of our friendship!

Gator Gets Me Involved in Social Activism through Social Media (The Early Days of My Internship as an

Urban Translator for United In Peace, INC)

I remember when Gator & myself was in a few Facebook Growth & Development groups & man talkin' about the chaos that would go on in those groups, it was a damn shame. I created the group along with a Brother by the name of Eric X "Stewart" (Nation of Islam / Growth & Development) by taking those same principles of Growth & Development we learned from the book *FROM GANGSTER DISCIPLE TO THE BLUEPRINT: GROWTH & DEVELOPMENT*. The group was becoming successful but someone got it shut down. Now with me being' an innovator, together with Eric X and Gator, We Created a group called the Better Ourself Society. I created a code of conduct for every member to sign & be an active member in that group. The group was created to teach, & enlighten brothers & sisters to help them become positive & productive people in their communities focusin' on EDUCATION, ECONOMICS, POLITICS, and SOCIAL DEVELOPMENT. This same group WE started which was to help others progress did the same for me. Through that same group, Better Ourself Society, I was introduced to another dear friend of Gator; a powerful & prolific Sister by the name of Maleta Kimmons aka Queen Nuchie. When she was first added to the group I didn't know who she was by face but I remembered her from a powerful documentary, *The Noonie G Story: Gangster with a Heart of Gold*, in 2007. I saw Gator greet her & he said the name "Queen Nuchie," and I'm thinkin' to myself like, "Hold up that's the same Sista in The Noonie G Story. If she good wit' Gator then she 100 wit' me." So, I inboxed her on FaceBook & we been tight ever since. She has helped me out a lot. She also introduced me to another mutual friend of her & Gator, my dear friend Mr. Bryan Crenshaw 'G. F. (GodFather).' He's currently in the Federal Institution doin' a life sentence. Queen Nuchie helped to mode & shape me like a mother & Gator was like my father & they kept me on point!

I remember when Bro. Eric X approached me with an idea of starting our first BlogTalkRadio show. Folks was like "bruh you gotta voice & a message that needs to be heard alongside of Min. Farrakhan & The Old man. You're a young Gator Bradley fam, We know He's groomin' you... It's time to be heard Folks." I told 'em, "I'mma see what Gator say first but it's cool wit' me jack." So Me & Bro. Eric came up with the name, *Born GOD Made Gangsta*. I hit Gator up about the idea; he was thrilled & said, "Hell Yeah that's the move that's what we suppose to be on." So, that let me know that was his blessing. From there *Born GOD Made Gangsta* was born & Gator was our 1st guest &

became a regular on that show. *Born GOD Made Gangsta*, also introduced me to Spike Moss. When I started workin' with One Family One Community (Founded by Maleta Kimmons "Queen Nuchie" & Bryan Crenshaw 'G.F.') more closely they started sponsoring *Born GOD made Gangsta*. We had a few issues that slowed the progress of the show & we started a new show with the same message called *Awareness 2 Conscious Minds*, created by Maleta & myself which was still sponsored by One Family One Community. As always, Gator was willin' & ready to participate. That was the beginning of Gator passing the torch on my road to becoming an Urban Translator. Gator had shown me that you must be Socially Active from Social Media to the reality of the Streets and Community.

A True Sign of Trust & Friendship

I remember back in November of 2011, I was invited (due to my first show *Born GOD Made Gangsta*) to Minnesota by Maleta & Spike Moss for the National Youth Justice Peace Summit sponsored by Uhuru Solutions & One Family One Community. I also had the pleasure of meeting Khalid Samaad at this summit. Gator was also invited but wasn't able to make it to the Summit. I remember Queen Nuchie had been tellin' me how out of control Minnesota had gotten due to the senseless foolishness. I wasn't scared, "Hell, I'm from Birmingham were niggaz don't give a damn!" I thought to myself. I told her & Gator I'm still comin' regardless. I kept in touch with Gator while I was there & kept him informed about what was goin' on. Well it turned out Nuchie was right like hell; It was way outta control. In the time I was there (2 days) I spoke the Summit and I went to a funeral of one of the Brothers with Nuchie & a guy who was at the summit, him & his wife was shot & killed. So when I talked to Gator I told 'em, "Nuchie was straight up tellin' tha truth...Mane they wide open buck wild as hell outta control jack! If & when you do come down (to Minnesota) you'll already know tha business on wuzz happenin.'" So a few weeks later a guy named K.G. Wilson invited Gator to Minneapolis, MN to speak at his 911 Peace Conference. Now I'm tellin' you this is how I knew Gator trusted me as a dear friend. I was back home in Alabama when he went to Minneapolis; he sent me his flight arrangements and his whole itinerary. He called me every hour on the hour to let me know who he was with and where he was at from the time he got up 'til time he laid down, until the time he went back home to Chicago.

Gator, myself & God Almighty knew his whereabouts at all times; plus, his wife & children. If that isn't a true sign of trust in a friend then I don't know what is!

A Meeting Face to Face (The Teacher Meets the Student: No Longer An Interim Urban Translator, Now I've Been Certified By The Master Urban Translator Mr. Wallace "Gator" Bradley, Himself)

I thank God for the day when I finally got to meet Gator face-to-face aside from phone calls & emails at the B.O.S. Weekend 2012 in Hattiesburg, MS. When Gator was interviewed for the May 17, 2012 edition of the *Final Call* he told me to call & give an account of what I saw when I was at the B.O.S. Weekend 2012. Even though the newspaper didn't use my piece I was honored that Gator thought about including' me. I called Gator that night after the *Final Call* interview and I told 'em, "I know what you doin' jack, you passin' me tha torch." His response was, "Damn right I am brothaman, yo' works speak for itself... Who not other than you." I smiled so hard & he went to tell me, "We gone have a picnic up here in a few months (Chicago). I wanna introduce you to some people & give you your certificate as a certified Urban Translator for United in Peace. Your internship is over now." I told my friends & family the news. I don't know who was happier me or them. Being an Urban Translator is very important in the community for the simple fact it's a bridge between the gap of urban & judicial politics it also keeps a strong presence of consciousness to the community. As Gator says, "We are all Urban Translators most of us has not realized it yet." Through working with Gator I've had the chance to work with Larry Hoover, Jr. & his mother as well as countless brothers & sisters across the country to help them find their purpose & keep the message of Growth & Development goin' strong by promoting Positive & Productive Outreach in the communities.

On June 23, 2012 in Birmingham, Alabama we had a *Stop The Violence March & Rally*. Gator and United In Peace, Inc. came to participate with The City of Birmingham due to the Senseless Violence. He also presented me with my Urban Translator Award Certificate at the 'March & Rally,' which made me official and the first Urban Translator since Mr. Bradley himself. Since then Mr. Bradley or as I like to call him, Uncle Gator, and I have worked closer than ever. We've worked with Birmingham City Councilman Jay Roberson of District 7 here in Birmingham, Al as participants in the *100 Days Of Nonviolence* event along with Elder Bernice King (daughter of Dr. Martin Luther King, Jr.) I gave Gator a tour of the historic Kelly Ingram Park and also the Historic Sixteenth Street Baptist Church where we all sat on the steps- Mr. Bradley thought the Church was destroyed by the bombings back in 1963.

Always Supportive & Positively Influential

In December of 2012, I ended my partnership at Alabama Hott Radio; and, in January 2013 decided to start my own Radio Station, Flame On Radio (www.flameonradio.com) along with DJ Firestarta (also a former partner in Alabama Hott Radio.) Gator & United In Peace was our first sponsor and major supporter. Gator was my first major call-in guest and always gave a word of Wisdom on my *show Live From The Streets with Lando Magic* which is a Hip Hop show that I have on my station. He's called in on *Chillin' @ Da Trap with DJ Firestarta & Lando Magic* quite a few times and also was a guest star on one of our newest shows to air, *Where They Do That At* hosted by Mz. Patience where Gator blew the minds of everybody who heard his words young and all. When Waka Flocka reached out to Gator and United in Peace, Inc. because he wanted to help the cause in stopping kids from killing one another, Gator made sure I was included and I got a chance to come to Chicago to see the Master Urban Translator at work and it was an eye opening experience.

One of the main reasons Gator's influence is so strong is because we come from the same walk of life, gangs & the street life... Though by the grace of God I've never been to prison & have no felony record, only through God's Grace's possible. Another reason is because Gator makes you always feel like family. He puts you in the mind of the cool ass uncle who don't play no games especially if it's on some foolishness, that wanna see you doin' right & good for yourself. He's a great person & the world needs to know more of his influence & allow him to go on to continue to touch others like me & countless others across the country. God Almighty & Mr. Larry Hoover Sr. lead & guide Gator Bradley to become a living testimony of Growth & Development which inspires me to do what I do as well as several Brothers & Sisters across this Country! Salute, to Wallace "Gator" Bradley. Gator has been a strong influence & helped me change my life for the better by leading by example. He's always supported me in all Righteous Endeavors & I was Honored that he asked me to be a part of this book. He's a blessing' from the Almighty Himself!

The best way to describe Gator Bradley is "Lead by example," & he does that to a tee. The impact that Gator has had on countless lives is truly a blessing. I am a part of the Murder to Excellence Movement. I live & speak Growth & Development for the H.A.M (Having A Moment in history) Generation. I am a registered voter and have been since I was 19yrs old; I encourage others to do the same. I truly believe in the Message of The Old Man (Larry Hoover Sr.) which is to Stop the senseless violence in our community... Stop the disrespect of our kids & elders of our community... That we are against the senseless robbing, raping & foolishness that goes on in our neighborhoods all across the country!

Like I said before, I was raised & baptized in the Civil Rights Movement so the Importance of OUR RIGHT TO VOTE is very inevitable. Our forefathers & mothers died for us to achieve the Right to vote & get a proper education and we should not let their struggle be in vain! There are individuals who wish they could have the right to vote & let their voice be heard and for those who are able not to register is a gotdamn shame. The power of the Vote is OURS by RIGHT. When Barack Obama was elected President 4yrs ago WE the Minorities made that happen by the Power of the Vote! When I engage in conversations I inform them, "By the power of the vote don't jus' don't put the President in office, it puts the Senate & Congress who will help or break the President in getting' this country on its feet in office. It's your vote on what Bill get's turned into a Law, that the jobs & employment rate gets set up to standard or job cuts that get made when you elect your City, State, or Federal Representative. If you don't vote to help change that ain't no need to sit among yo'selves & complain about anything when you don't use your voice which is your vote!"

When Gator came to Hattiesburg, MS for B.O.S Weekend 2012 (which was the 10yr anniversary for the function) he pushed the same message titled as this book *MURDER to EXCELLENCE: Growth and Development for The H.A.M (Having A Moment in history) [Millennial] GENERATION*, which encourages Brothers & Sisters to register to vote, get others registered and help felons get their rights to vote back. The message is also to be pillars & peace keepers of the community by helping to fight against the senseless foolishness that goes on our communities and to help rebuild that Economic dollar back into our communities where we can do for ourselves. As Gator said, "We askin' you to put down them pistols & pick up a picket sign… We askin' you to trade in them bullets for a voter's ballot." And that's been the message Gator has always been on. That's like in the recent Political, Judicial event that the U.S. Supreme Court pretty much repealed The Voters Right Act of 1965. Mr. Bradley is still teaching the importance of Civil Rights & the Civil Rights Movement.

Gator has shown me when mainstream media don't give us an outlet make one so the message gets out there clearly. We've been pushin' the song *Murder to Excellence* by Kanye West & Jay Z, it's a powerful song with a message about the senseless violence in our communities and

Mainstream Radio won't touch the song... but God is so good & lets everything happen for a reason! I used my influence at Alabama Hott Radio.com & on May 22, 2012 We aired *Murder to Excellence* on *Chillin' @ Da Trap w/ DJ Firestarta* & air it every time we go on air! Even now that I have Flame On Radio which is my own station *Murder To Excellence* by Kanye west & Jay Z is a song that is in full spin rotation. Mainstream Radio & Internet Radio Stations still refuse to touch that song now because of its Righteous Message. Gator always calls me, "A Social Media Conglomerate Genius." I truly believe in the words James Brown wrote to a song back in 1969, "I don't want nobody to give me nothin' open up tha door & I'll get it myself." Gator influenced me to use the internet since mainstream media ain't gone give us the chance to do it. Since everyone is on the internet why not use it to promote the message of Peace, Love,& Unity in our Community?! Whether it be through internet talk shows or internet Hip Hop radio, the message of truth will be put out there... The truth can no longer be hidden!

A Brief Summary About My Trip to Chicago to See the Master Urban Translator

On June 8, 2013 I came to Chicago, IL. I was invited by Gator to participate as an Urban Translator for United in Peace, Inc. and also as a representative for my radio station and staff for Flame on Radio due to Waka Flocka & Brick Squad Monopoly reaching out to United in Peace, Inc. along with Museum 44 "Where Hip Hop meets History" for the *Street Order Tour* which was supposed to been held on June 10, 2013. I had a chance to get an inside scoop on situations and details leading up to that event which was postponed. I witnessed Gator speaking up and out for Waka Flocka wanting to change his life and that nobody should look down on him for wanting to do the right thing. I saw Gator go head to head with publicists & Chicago News Media in regards to Waka Flocka wanting to go to the Schools in Chicago and speak to the kids about stopping the senseless violence and shootings going on in Chicago's Schools. I watched how Gator fought tooth and nail to get Waka's people to understand how important it is for Waka to talk to the kids about stopping the violence. I also saw that he's highly loved and respected by the people in the communities of Chicago. Like when I first arrived in Chicago at the Greyhound station, a few people asked me who up in Chicago I'm coming to see. I told one Gentleman I'm visiting my Uncle on a Peace Concert. When he asked who my Uncle was I told him Gator Bradley. Well that Gentlemen made sure I needed nothing, when I ran low on Cigarettes waiting on my ride he gave me his. Not to mention, he stayed with me until Gator arrived at the Greyhound station to pick me up. Even though the event got postponed until July- which I missed- My experience in Chicago with Gator was a great educational one, like I gave him when He came to Birmingham. I also saw that Gator is a Man who can't be bought, he can't be sold, he can't be corrupted because he came from the streets which are full of corruption and greed. He overcame it all and influences young and old to be Positive & Productive people in the Community which is a blessing in itself. I am just grateful for Mr. Bradley for being such a strong positive blessing in my life and showing me the way or as Gator says "Passin' the torch."

Goals and Inspiration of the Book MURDER to EXCELLENCE: Growth & Development for the H.A.M (Having A Moment in history)

The book, *MURDER to EXCELLENCE: Growth and Development for The H.A.M (Having A Moment in history) [Millennial] GENERATION, The Autobiography of Wallace "Gator" Bradley, Urban Translator* will be a powerful & prolific testimony of what it really means to live Growth & Development. This book will help continue to save lives as Gator's work has in the Past, does in the Present, & will for Future generations who read this book. I am deeply honored and privileged to be featured in this book and to have the opportunity to give an account on Wallace 'Gator' Bradley's influence on my life- as he has influenced others. All Praises Due To the Most High.

Thank You and GOD Bless,

Orlando "Lando Magic" Henry

SAFE PASSAGE

I first encountered Gator in Ada Park which is located in Morgan Park; a neighborhood on the far south side of Chicago. The year was 1977; Gator and approximately 30 of his soldiers were located on the southeast corner of the park. Gator was a Gangster Disciple involved in a customary ritual of physically disciplining his disobedient soldiers. The southeast corner of Ada Park was my gateway home which meant that I unfortunately had to cross paths with Gator and these nefarious characters. Gator ceased his attitude adjustment session, separated the circle and called me to the center of this hostile group of gang-bangers. Gator then declared and articulated an unwritten "street code" which prohibited gang-bangers from intimidating, threatening, or physically harming senior citizens, children, athletes, or any child carrying a musical instrument. At the end of his proclamation, Gator told me to run home. That was the first and last time I followed the directives of a gang-banger. I now recognize Gator as the first person to institute "safe passage" in the Morgan Park community. I was certainly grateful.

My next encounter with Gator occurred in 2012. Again, he told me to run. However, this time I was running for a seat as a Judge of the Circuit Court of Cook County. Gator had previously served his debt to society in one of Illinois' penal institutions and subsequently received a pardon from the Governor of Illinois. Remorseful, redeemed and now respected; Gator served as a consultant in my 2013 judicial campaign. Affectionately known as the Urban Interpreter, Gator's immense knowledge of the political landscape and his unique character is valued from the Oak Park to Morgan Park. Gator ushered and introduced our campaign to a variety of individuals from different segments of our diverse society. Thanks to the efforts of Gator, and numerous volunteers, we won our election by an impressive margin of approximately 64% of the votes. I express my sincere gratitude to Wallace "Gator" Bradley. He is the epitome of a man who worked his way from the streets to the suites.

Carl B. Boyd

One thing that I know about Wallace 'Gator' Bradley is that he is a fighter, a champion, and a hero. Without his involvement in the anti-violence movement we would have more violence in Chicago and other parts of this country. In the 1990's Gator was one of the driving forces behind the peace treaty and nationwide peace summit held in Chicago, which helped reduce gang violence. Gator has a unique set of skills, he is and urban archeologist, anthropologist and paleontologist, so he knows his way around when it comes to gangs and their habits. There is a misconception among policing bodies about Gator; they really need a person like Gator to help give them a non-traditional view of the gang problem. Like Gator, the system knows that crime and violence is only a symptom of a larger problem, basically socio-economic. When the economic level is low in an area then crime and violence is high, but when the economic level is high in an area then violence is low and it don't take a rocket scientist to figure it out. Gator's unique ability to communicate with the street element sets him apart from all others. Like Gator, I believe in community laws and certain things cannot and will be tolerated in the community.

Remember this if you don't remember anything else, Gator has put his life and family on the line. Not many men would do that. – Your Friend, **Hal Baskin**

The Autobiography of Wallace Gator Bradley, Urban Translator

As a veteran activist of over 40 years on local, state, and national levels, I am pleased to say that for over 30 years I have known and worked with Wallace "Gator" Bradley and with him we worked personally and professionally together from Harold Washington as first Black Mayor of Chicago to Barack Obama as the first Black President of the United States. I have personally witnessed the trials of Bradley as he worked from the streets, to the suites, and even the alleys of Chicago and across the country working to carry out the challenge given to him by Larry Hoover to transform the GD from Gangster Disciples street gang to GD of Growth and Development into mainstream society, and Bradley has done just that.

I worked with Gator very close during the 1988 Presidential Campaign for Rev. Jesse Jackson where I was one of the National Youth Coordinators and Bradley joined our grassroots national field team. I watched how Gator used his former negative street gang skills in a constructive way to reach ex-offenders, at-risk youth and other disengaged constituencies in Chicago and across the country. Long before he coined the title of "urban translator," he was doing just that by translating what the urban agenda of Rev. Jackson's campaign meant to lifting up those voters at the bottom who had no hope and Gator was right there engaging them into registering and voting. Since that 1988 campaign to today Wallace "Gator" Bradley has worked tirelessly at getting ex-offenders and other grassroots citizens to use his example of turning from the gang, drug and other illegal street activities into good citizens. We worked together on the original historic Chicago Gang/Peace Summit and I watched as Gator and others risked their lives trying to bring about peace. It was Gator who successfully helped to work at achieving the first major gang truce in Cabrini Green housing developments.

From all these efforts I watched how others had predicted that Gator would not be able to sustain himself trying to live a legitimate life, but he has continually proved the critics wrong continuing to achieve with his advocacy work empowering thousands of former gang members and others from negative to positive lifestyles. And after Gator received his official pardon/clemency from the Illinois Governor, he went to work yet again learning how to turn his advocacy into a legal business entity, the United in Peace Organization. His professionalism for how citizens worked with government came directly from the blessings and experiences Gator received from the entry level job from the legendary Jerry "Iceman" Butler, Cook County Commissioner. From that experience with Jerry Butler to all the connections he received from the Rev. Jesse Jackson and others, Gator Bradley has used them all in his ongoing work locally to nationally and the issue of peace in the urban streets.

He continues to handle the criticism of promoting the behind the wall messages of Larry Hoover, but Gator remains committed and focused on showing that he is a real example of one who came out of the environment of being gang enforcer for Larry Hoover in environments of murder to a new committed life of excellence as a good citizen, and a life where he continues to promote the fact that his life turned around for the better because of the urging of Larry Hoover to use the Hoover name as one that promotes the negative elements from Gangster Disciple to one of Growth and Development. While everyone who used to be a member of the negative elements of the Hoover organization may have not followed the new Hoover direction, Wallace "Gator" Bradley is certainly one that stands out as a real example of transforming his life from environments of 'Murder To Excellence' and indeed he continues to be a national model of further transformation from a leader of Gangster Disciple to a leader of Growth and Development.

I want to thank Wallace "Gator" Bradley for asking me to even write a few words to be included but he insisted for over 30 years I have been a direct partner in his growth and development and all the hell he has been through and continues to face despite his successes. I am glad to say that going forward into the next chapter of Gator's life that we are committed to staying connected personally and professionally through his organization, United in Peace, and through mine with The National Black Wall Street Chicago and National Black Wall Street USA movements. Our next chapter will be showing the Black community that it has the collective economic power to put our people to work and erase their need to be caught up in gang, drug and other illegal economies. So here is to the next chapter for Wallace "Gator" Bradley's life and may this current book be an ongoing life lesson for others to follow.

Mark S. Allen
Veteran Activist
Chairman, National Black Wall Street Chicago

Wallace "Gator" Bradley has been a mentor, role model and an extended uncle to me since I was young. Coming from a single parent home my Mother did all she could to raise a Man but ONLY a Man can teach a Boy to become a Man. From keeping me safe and out of trouble as a youth to encouraging and guiding me and keeping me focused in College, "Gator," has been nothing but an inspiration in my life. I am so thankful to God for placing him in my life at a young age. Now as a Man I understand why he was so hard on me growing up and can see the results of the many lessons now.

David A. Peterson, Jr.
President, A. Phillip Randolph Pullman Porters Museum

Wallace "Gator" Bradley, the Urban Translator, President of United In Peace Inc. organization, Community Activist, legal advocate and foremost "Free Larry Hoover" spokesman is no less than a miracle of human transformation.

Brother Gator would be the first one to tell you, "I'm not a saint, I'm just a black man trying to do what I know is right so that our children won't have to carry the burden of what we did wrong." "What I do is not really for us, it's for our children and the yet unborn."

Former Enforcer for the notorious GD (Gangster Disciple) street organization Chief (Larry Hoover) is now 100% committed to solving the most glaring problems within the Black community through prudent, socio-political strategies within the very system he once loved to hate.

A loving husband, committed father, loyal friend and brother, Wallace Gator Bradley is a man of many productive layers. He is an Urban Translator, Mentor and teacher to many men and women. We honor him for his work within African-American communities nationally and work diligently under his skillful tutelage to become Urban Translators ourselves.

Wallace Gator Bradley brilliantly assesses a problem, conceives the solution, publically articulates the cause, promotes the movement, heralds the call, recruits the concerned and then it's on.

Fortified with incurable optimism, no matter how aggressively certain media spokespersons and other haters may attempt to minimize his efforts and focus on his past, Brother Gator chooses to accept it as free publicity and continues to move forward keeping his focus on the goal ahead.

I have been privileged to be Wallace Gator Bradley's web designer. We started with the first website, www.unitedinpeaceinc.org; then, we developed thebradleyreport.unitedinpeaceinc.org. Our newest project is the www.freelarryhoovernow.org website.

Gator is more than a client. He is a mentor, brother and friend. Working with Gator on various projects has been and continues to be the most exciting and meaningful work that I do. I am blessed to be a part of the United In Peace, Inc. organization as an Urban Translator/Internet Marketing Specialist.

This book is timely and prayerfully will inspire many people to do their part in the uplifting of a fallen humanity. Wallace Gator Bradley is a man who has courage enough for truth. And in his unique way, inspires us to contribute to the making of a better world for us all.

I wish him much success!

>Sincerely,
>
>**Kevin Clay-El**
>**September 13, 2013**

The Autobiography of Wallace Gator Bradley, Urban Translator

My name is Denise Carter, in the streets I am known as Sister Loyal, Loyal G, or the newest nickname the Sisters and Brothers hung up on me... Sistah Souljah.

I grew up on the south side of the inner city of Kalamazoo Michigan. Growing up all I seen and heard was about Larry Hoover and the GD's. I was actively communicating with members on a daily basis, I was maybe around 12 years old. The image of the GDs the media put out wasn't what I experienced at all, they showed me love; they taught me that we were making a change, we had a voice and they freed my mind from mental slavery at an early age. By the time I was 16 years old I was involved in community clean-ups, doing community service in nursing homes, and learning about voting. I was the only female and most definitely stood out because I amwhite according the the government's standards, but I am really a mix of German and Native American, but nonetheless I stood out.

In 1996, June 21st to be exact, I met my Big Brother, and the first person he spoke to me about was Gator Bradley, and the movement he has to bring peace to the streets. He also spoke to me about how important my education was, how my voice matters and if I applied myself I could reach many people he couldn't. I began to pay attention to local and world politics. I started to notice the lack of equality, the police brutality, the mental slavery and how the media got rich from our self destruction.

I continued to speak out and give back, but it seemed my voice wasn't being heard. So, in 2010 I moved to GA I started networking with people online (something new for me), Ifound several people like myself, anti racism, humanitarians, revolutionist, fighters the stop violence and police brutality. I had a strong network by 2011. I was actively putting together 'feed the community events' with those I networked with, often doing fund raisers and putting in money on my own. I started a group called the community diversity program in 2012, it consisted of various street organizations coming together to clean up the community and feed the hungry, we collected clothes for the kids and canned goods for the food pantries. I then began going to the City Hall to meet with the Mayor and City Manager in Dublin, Georgia. My goal was to start a recovery program for inmates re-entering society and support groups for both reformed gang members and former inmates, I am still working on this program.

Also in 2012, I had been working closely with several stop the violence groups and by now I had been mentored by Orlando Henry for over a year. I also had been working with Gator Bradley via phone for several months. I was actively on the P.O.P.S Council and a faithful follower of the guidance of Noble Ameer Ali. I took the tools and skills I had developed from these great men and sat down and put together a peace treaty to address a conflict that had arisen between organizations in Midgeville, Georgia.

I used the 6 steps to peace from P.O.P.S, and a basic format of a peace treaty Brother Andre Hester structured some years before for HaysState prison, I changed it and fine tuned it to fit the people and their issues in this case. I called Brother Orlando and told him what I was about to do, he gave me sound advice, encouragement and told me I would be fine, just be myself and speak from the heart.

After my conversation with Brother Orlando, I contacted the Leaders of both parties and set up a meeting a local restaurant, I made sure the atmosphere was professional and organized yet comfortable for everyone, two sisters Arrie Freeney and O. Jones, accompanied me to the meeting. I was very humbly surprised when all parties showed up, I greeted everyone with love, we sat down and I started off by asking how everyone was and how they felt. Once it was confirmed they were ok and felt comfortable I laid out the rules of conduct that would be accepted and expected, once agreed upon. I explained to party 1 (Crips) what the concern was and how this was affecting the community and causing an unsafe environment for not only the elderly but also the children. BLUE this is the name of the man I was speaking to explained to me that he didn't know a lot of what I told him was going on, he also explained that a lot of the problem was personal feelings from years before when the GDs in that city were not so humble. Both sides spoke to each other openly expressing a lack of positive guidance and knowledge years back, but both sides agreed violence is not what they wanted.

I pulled out the 6 steps to peace which I had also altered to fit this specific case, andshowed it to them, in it was a detailed way to communicate with each other, how to identify an issue before it occurs and how to stop and correct the issue before it got out of control, both parties liked the steps and agreed to exercise those steps. In the peace treaty it stated before any action would be taken towards violence the parties would come together and talk and then and come to an agreement and each party would be responsible for the redirection of their own members. They agreed that in 30 days I would return and we would meet again and see how things were going and fine tune anything that wasn't working.

The Autobiography of Wallace Gator Bradley, Urban Translator

When I returned not only were things going very well but Blue was sitting on the porch with a gentleman from the other party having a drink and talking about politics amongst the two parties. They told me things were great, no issues at all. It has been several months, I talk to both parties often and the two parties have literally been incident free since the peace treaty signing and they assist each other in community events.

In 2013, I read a status United in Peace posted about Larry Hoover. There was a photo attached and in the photo Larry Hoover had on overalls, the photo's caption spoke about agriculture, and how we should learn to grow our own food, and many other valuable pieces of information, but that part along with the photo caught my eye, I thought what a great way to bridge the gap, we can start an URBAN Garden and let the small kids and teenagers learn from the community elders! I spoke with Brother Gator who put me in contact withBrother Bentley in Chicago, he told me a basic plan on how to start the garden where to get help and how to find a location. Myself, Curtis Thomas (Doughboy) and two children, Nyima and Tyler went to the City Hall in Cochran, GA to present the idea. Things went very well when I spoke and told them of the idea. The mayor suggested places to start it, the council offered to help work the garden and the community members offered seeds and advice, we allowed the children to speak on how they felt about the idea and of course meet the mayor. We found a place for the garden, in an unfortunate turn of events the property was given to someone else the day we set to break ground. We have been looking for a new location and to our happy surprise we have found a new location a nd plan to start planting very soon.

In January of 2013, a young man's story was brought to my attention, his name is Kendrick Johnson, he is a 17yr old black male that was found dead in his school gym. He hadn't came home from school January 9th, his family was worried and reported that he did not come home. The next day January 10th, KJ's lifeless body was found rolled up and upside down in a gym mat. His body had been discovered and local police were on the scene several hours before the coroner was ever notified, the scene had been compromised, his face severely disfigured, it was not recognizable, his face has been compared to that of Emmett Till. Along with the suspected story not the one the police tried to tell, the family was not allowed to see KJ's body until January 13th, days had went by. At the time my car had broke down, I could not travel, but I knew KJ's cousin Kim Green, I asked her to please tag me in all posts, new

information and all actions concerning the case, the
Internet was my only tool besides the phone. I called Gato
r and told him about this young man and he told me to
continue following the story and gave me his blessing and
guidance on how to help. I also contacted Orlando Henry
and told him about this young man and he jumped
right on it with me and helped me bring awareness to KJ. I
called CNN, the local news, and the local police station. I
posted and reposted every piece of information about him
I found. I spoke to his father and got his input on the
matter and his blessing to help. Awareness did start to
happen, through group efforts. Many months went by
before the official autopsy report came back saying it
was an accidental death, this caused an uproar. Soon after
many protests, news reports and Al Sharpton getting
involved, KJ was exhumed and a second autopsy
was done. The results are still not in, and this movement
THE KJ MOVEMENT, is still strong. I encourage
everyone to Google and YouTube any information you ca
n find out about Kendrick Johnson 17 yrs old Valdosta,
GA found January 10th 2013.

Also in 2013, there was a violent act of shooting in a
local park in Lagrange, GA. Several people were injured
and yes there were some deaths. At the time, myself and
several of those in my network of people were planning to

do a Switch Lanes event; we decided to do the event at the location of the shooting in Lagrange, myself and about 13 people from various cities (Growth and Development) came together and grilled food had games and gave out cards and necklaces handmade and donated to that community from the inmates within the GA prison system. Although the event was not a huge one, people returned to the park, this is something they had been afraid to do A news reporter came out and interviewed us and took photos, at the end of the day, the kids, and teenagers where playing basketball, water balloon fights and had full bellies, and we had a feeling of happiness, we plan on going back soon to do it again.

I have got to give credit to Allah first for all the blessings I have been given and received, Brother Gator for his dedication and words of wisdom, I look up to you, Orlando for grooming me and molding me with care patience and love. Noble Ameer Ali your wisdom is never ending, you never fail to enlighten me and feed my soul love to you, and the entire United in Peace Family, thank you for being my guiding light and letting my voice be heard, for an unconditional love I can only hope to one day repay.

And a special thank you to a man I like to call my Father (he has been one to me for years through his words of wisdom and teachings of righteousness) Larry Hoover, thank you for the Vision, the love you instilled in me, for teaching about righteousness and community unity, and most of all giving me the tools and skills to free-your-Dome (my dome) so that I was able to be free of mental slavery.

In love and service (Urban Translator)
Denise "Loyal G" Carter

My Name is Bro. Ronnie D. Hawkins Jr. and I was born and raised in Dumas, Arkansas. I started believing in the (GROWTH & DEVELOPMENT) teachings of our Great Visionary and Honorable Chairman Bro. Larry Hoover In 1994, who is also the founder of United in Peace Incorporated. In 2009, I wanted to get more involved with community outreach and I wanted to give my personal testimony to the youth of how the Vision of the Hon. Larry Hoover and the teachings of the Society of Growth and Development inspired me to make a positive change in my life.

This same year (2009) I created a Facebook account, through this account I found and reached out to the Hon. Bro. Wallace "Gator" Bradley, the President and Secretary of United In Peace, Inc. who taught me about the beneficent nonprofit and private foundation of United in Peace Inc. United in Peace, Inc. directly mentored and influenced me to get actively involved in the Betterment of Our Cities, Towns, Communities and the entire country and to make a lifetime commitment to help Stop the Violence, senseless shootings, the disrespect and rape of our women and the disrespect and robbery of the elderly and senior citizens. I have we been working hard (volunteering) to help uplift communities across the

country ever since as an official "URBAN TRANS-
LATOR" for United In Peace, Inc. To God Be the
Glory!!! AMEN!!!

**BRO. RONNIE HAWKINS
AND UNITED IN PEACE, INC.
"THE OUTREACH AND UPLIFTING ACTS"...**

21 FROM 'THE BLUEPRINT'

[The Forks of Life or crossed 'pitchforks' are described in Growth & Development as representing "a crossroad." This is a conceptual evolution from their original meaning under the Gangster Disciple designation. Following is an abridged version of the chapter *"Forks of Life,"* excerpted from, *From Gangster Disciple to Growth & Development: The Blueprint* by Rod Emery and Larry Hoover, Sr. (1996). It does not reflect the full content or context of the book.]

Upon being introduced to the teachings of GROWTH and DEVELOPMENT, we find ourselves at a crossroad in our lives.

Under the "old concept," the crossed forks represented a negative way of life. We "crossed 'em up" on our chest in order to show allegiance to a gang's turf. We tattooed the crossed forks on our arms, chest, etc., in order to show a rebellious, defiant attitude toward society's laws and rules. We boldly stated that we were outlaws belonging to a criminal "mob." Many have killed and died representing the negative aspect of the crossed forks. Some of us even went as far as to believe the crossed forks were the sign of evil. They are not. However, such a negative view and insane belief justified our passion in the execution of crime. Now it is time to turn all this around and LIVE according to the true meaning of THE FORKS OF LIFE.

Under the "New Concept," the Forks of Life represent the physical and spiritual (mental) sides of man. Our teachings are universal in the sense that everyone on earth is confronted with crossroads throughout his or her life. Have you ever heard the proverbial saying, "A fork in the road?" Well, when people use that term they are talking about a crossroad in his or her life.

The Forks of Life represent the crossroads in our lives from the beginning to the end. Growth and development in the beginning of one's life is natural and unimpeded. At birth, the power to grow and develop is instilled in us and nurtured and stimulated by our environment. The first level of growth and development begins in our mother's womb. The cells join and unfold until what emerges is a fully formed child. From that point, quite naturally and without effort on our part, the various crossroads of life succeed one another. Once born, the baby begins to focus his eyes, to reach out and touch things, to move things around if possible, making sounds that he discovers causes others to respond (like crying for milk, laughing for affection.) Soon he confronts the challenge of sitting up (a crossroad), walking (a crossroad) and finally talking (a most difficult crossroad.) All people everywhere have had to succeed the challenge of these crossroads. They are only stages in one's growth and development; stages we all had to meet and overcome in order to survive…

Often, being in jail represents a crossroad. You begin to realize that it's time to make a change. But as crossroads go, you are given two ways from which to choose; the positive and negative. You can become deeply enmeshed in the causes that landed you in jail, or you can begin to pay attention to that inner voice (your conscience) that is telling the right way to go. We must realize that when we choose negative over positive we help to sustain prison as BIG business. In other words, when we choose not to live according to the "new Concept" we guarantee ourselves a negative life; a life filled with death incarceration.

We are confronted with crossroads before we go to prison, jail or death. Nobody is born a criminal. At some point in our life, we were confronted with the decision of "picking up that gun," "dealing those drugs," "robbing that person or store" or "breaking into that home or business." At the very moment that we are confronted with the decision to do something wrong, we are also given the opportunity to decide what is right. Any such situation represents a crossroad and that is what the crossed forks represent, the many crossroads in one's life…

... It is more than merely changing the name from "Gangster Disciples" to "GROWTH and DEVELOPMENT." Rather, it is a change from evil to good; from negative to positive; from secret to open; from hidden to unhidden; from illiterate to literate; and from the "old concept" to the New Concept. Our six principles are pushing us at breath-taking speed to prepare us for the changes which our education and past experiences have failed to help us realize. The ability to handle the difficulties involved in such changes lie within ourselves; that is to say, in our attitude toward these changes...

The kind of change that the Forks of Life represent, the kind that all alone can ensure our survival, is personal Growth and Development; Growth and Development of talents, of relationships, of love and loyalties, Growth and Development of a capacity to see and hear more deeply the true meanings of life. Growth and Development in these areas change individuals and organizations and can free us for more courageous and competent action in all areas of our lives. When we continue to grow and develop and maintain our capacity for change and openness, the hope of our future generations is contained within the Forks of Life...

Finally, the Forks of Life represent our physical and spiritual (mental) strength. Each prong of the forks upholds a particular principle. Whenever we are confronted with a challenging situation such as changing our lifestyle, the Forks of Life represent the strength that we can find in studying and applying our six principles. The Forks of Life bear witness to the many struggles (crossroads) that life confronts us with. However, more than anything else, the Forks of Life symbolize our constant forward thrust.

Armed with Love, Life, Loyalty, Knowledge, Wisdom and Understanding resting upon the prongs of the Forks of Life, we push forward into society, not to destroy but to build.

[The following is abridged from, *From Gangster Disciple to Growth & Development: The Blueprint* by Rod Emery and Larry Hoover, Sr. (1996). It does not reflect the full content or context of the book or 'The Six Principles of Growth & Development.']

Love

Love is the one creative force of all existence.

Love surpasses all other principles because it is the first cause of the creation of humanity. Simply put, without love there would be no you. Thus, love can make certain that we progress non-stop toward educational, economical, political and social development and pave the way for our necessary change into the New Concept. First we must give our life's energy to love for each other. All else is secondary. Therefore, we are faced with the question, "Am I my brother's keeper?" Love asks us not to ignore the shortcomings of our fellow brothers of the struggle, but to love him in spite of his shortcomings; to show faith in the love within him that he will catch our leadership's vision and in time come to realize his own strength and seek to rise above our past. We need not flatter him nor lead him to over-estimate himself. Rather, we should help him to understand himself and know that he has a friend who will aid and assist him in 'righteous endeavors.' To that degree, we are our brother's keeper.

Life

Life is the creative force of love in action.

Life is energy that grows and develops toward a particular purpose. When you are not growing and developing toward a purpose, you are dying or dead. Life is the pure energy that flows through all creation. It flows through animals and plants, as well as humans. It flows through the physical and mental, as well as the spiritual. Life is the pure energy that flows through every animated object in the universe, known and unknown. The energy that it takes for a thought to be made into a reality is the same energy that it takes to walk, one foot before the other. Life is energy in its purest form. The life that lives in the core of an atom is the same energy that gave birth to all creation. All energy (all life) is part and parcel of one creative force. However, life is governed by laws, which means you will only get from life that which you put into it.

A person's life-style is simply the way in which he uses his creative force (his life's energy). Lifestyles can be destructive or constructive to the creative force within you.

Whatever attitudes, thoughts or emotions that we create in one moment, we carry to the next moment. We must disconnect ourselves from those lifestyles that will only create negative results in our lives. We must involve ourselves in the positive expressions of life. We must take charge and creatively direct our own lives into the Divine visions of our leadership.

Loyalty

Loyalty is service and cooperation with an organized scheme of things.

The best in life is ours, not at the expense of our fellow man but in accordance with our loyalty to an organized scheme of things. Loyalty is the natural result of being in-tune (in cooperation) with our purpose for living. Loyalty is necessary for the accomplishment of our goals and objectives. We have one mind, one aim and one purpose. This is true loyalty, true service and true cooperation.

Those of us who want to reflect a true and positive purpose in life must give our life to loyalty for a true and positive purpose. Those of us who want to reflect true love must give our loyalty to that which we truly love. Those of us who want to reflect a good life must give our loyalty to the good things in life. Most importantly, those of us who wish to reflect the New Concept must give our undying loyalty to that which is to be accomplished by the New Concept. Therefore, we must begin to build (within our communities) a disciplined group of people who are capable of adding momentum to our struggle by living according to our principles.

Our loyalty can grow and develop through our service and cooperation to the New Concept. True loyalty can only be developed through that which we believe in. It cannot be forced, but neither can true be destroyed by outside forces. Service and cooperation gives birth to inner-peace and a true understanding of loyalty. We must project our sense of loyalty to those things that are positive for the community.

Knowledge
Knowledge is the ability to Grow and Develop through study, observation and application.

As we cultivate the ability to discriminate between
the right and wrong, knowledge, we are reaching that level of existence where we can become masters of our own destiny.

For us to acquire knowledge of what is proper for our

physical appetites is a physical awakening. As we begin to practice the proper knowledge for our purpose, we will have a mental awakening. When we are able to understand that knowledge which can manifest our true inner desires, our ideals; we will have a spiritual awakening.

There are three basic ways of acquiring knowledge, through study, through observation and through application (actual experience). Study that which you know is the proper knowledge for our purpose, observe those who best reflect your highest ideal, and create the attitude that will allow you to apply (experience) that which you have studied, observed and found to be proper for our purpose. It is through knowledge that we convey our level of intelligence to the world. The proper knowledge is that which will allow us to present ourselves as needed and wanted in our communities and the world. The proper knowledge for our purpose can forge the New Concept into an accelerating movement of people (both young and old), with not only the desire, but the tools to become "a reckoning power of people."

Knowledge is the opposite of illiteracy. As we begin to grow and develop in the proper knowledge, we automatically begin to eliminate its opposite, illiteracy. By the same token, as long as we postpone pursuing the proper knowledge for our purpose, we are defending our state of illiteracy. The law does not change. With your every action, you are breaking a law or defending a law. If you are not defending our quest for knowledge then you are defending its opposite, illiteracy.

Illiteracy has been used to turn the burning hostility of poor people against one another. As a result, crime is high and rampant throughout society but especially in the poor communities (Black on Black, poor on poor crimes are becoming epidemic). This condition of rising crime has been exploited by the powers that be in order to pressure society into accepting this generation of poor/ Black youth as being Class X human beings. Our communities are being led to believe that if this generation of poor/ Black youth is X-ed out of existence, the problem of rising crime will be eliminated. Our New Concept teaches us that such thinking is genocidal in its nature and application. Therefore, our goals as individuals should be to wholeheartedly combat illiteracy be re-educating ourselves with the proper knowledge for our purpose (which is Growth & Development).

The proper knowledge will allow us to grow beyond this condition and communicate to our communities that we are not the problem. Rather, we are the effect of a problem that was caused long before we were born. Our problem is that we did not have knowledge of how we were (very subtly) being denied educationally, withheld economically, controlled politically and X-ed out socially. That is the problem! Our lack of knowledge about who, what, how and why this condition was created in the first place is the problem. Know the ledge by understanding cause and effect. That which is a problem for poor/ Black people could very well be the solution for rich people. To know the ledge is to know the cause and effect of any situation.

We must begin now to seek the proper knowledge needed for us to grow beyond these genocidal effects. Either we make a creative social response or die. It is time to lower our profile and begin the serious task of re-educating ourselves with the proper knowledge for our purpose.

Wisdom

Wisdom is knowledge applied wisely.

Wisdom is to understand that actions are not only the physical exertion of energy, but also the thoughts are actions too. Thought (like a new born baby) is born from the union of the mind and soul. A thought is "movement" of the mind. This "movement" can be constructive or destructive to the thinker. Regardless, in various degrees, all "movement" of the mind (thought) must manifest itself into the material world, if you will. In this manner, the action of our thoughts is that we continually become what we think. The true link between a physical action and a thought action is separated by 360 degrees. Our thoughts travel the same 360 degrees that our physical actions travel and like our physical actions, the act of thinking returns to us in the form of results, we become what we think. The result of our thoughts, not the intent, is the completion of its traverse on our 360 degree cycle of life and is recognized as what determines the rewards or afflictions allowed or disallowed us.

Wisdom demands that we become more broadminded and incorporate the understanding that even though people have different symbols, ceremonies, customs and beliefs, they are not less (nor more) human than we are. They deserve the same level of respect that we would demand from them.

Understanding

Understanding is the crowning point of all our principles.

Understanding is the most important because only through understanding can we become whole and complete our 360 degree cycle of educational, economical, political and social development. Through understanding we become whole because it (understanding) rejoins us to our first principle, (Love), and makes all the principles of our six-pointed star a platform upon which we can firmly stand.

['The Creed,' excerpted from, *From Gangster Disciple to Growth & Development: The Blueprint* by Rod Emery and Larry Hoover, Sr. (1996).]

We believe in the teachings of our Honorable Chairman:

ALL, as in ONE, we depend on, trust and have faith in, and are surrounded by the guidance and instruction coming from he who belongs to us as a worthy, noble, righteous, moral dignified and honest Leader, moderator and Master of THE VISION.

We believe in all laws and policies set forth by the Chairman and Executive Staff:

ALL, as in One, we depend on, trust and have faith in, and are surrounded by absolute rules of conduct as well as wise and practical decisions regarding our conduct in various situations, as decreed and determined through the message of our Leader, moderator and Master of THE VISION as well as those who put into effect, administer and execute the vision.

We believe in the concept and ideology of organization:

ALL, as in ONE, we depend on, trust and have faith in, and are surrounded by the thought, theory, opinion and view, as well as the philosophical disciplines and doctrines associated with, a unified and consolidated group of people with an executive structure that deals with the well being of all its people; an executive structure of business and enterprise for individual GROWTH & DEVELOPMENT and collective acceleration of the body as a whole.

We believe in aiding and assisting our fellow brothers in the struggle for all "RIGHTEOUS ENDEAVORS:"

ALL, as in ONE, we depend on, trust and have faith in, and are surrounded by the desire to support through friendship, as well as the desire to be cooperative toward those who belong to us as our companions and are allied to us by THE CREED and membership associated with our battle for GROWTH & DEVELOPMENT, and are concerned with everything in the area of moral and honorable undertakings of enterprise and livelihood.

We believe in standing strongly upon our six points utilizing KNOWLEDGE, WISDOM and UNDERSTANDING as we strive in our struggle for EDUCATIONAL, ECONOMICAL, POLITICAL and SOCIAL DEVELOPMENT.

ALL, as in ONE, we depend on, trust and have faith in, and are occupied and concerned with continuing to endure courageously by means of that which belongs to us as the six principles of GROWTH & DEVELOPMENT. We must make the most possible use of our ability to

GROW & DEVELOP through Study, Observation and Application, and our ability to apply, WISELY that which we have found to be true as well as our ability to look within and listen to and trust, that small inner voice that tells us the difference between right and wrong.

At the same time, ALL, as in ONE, must move forward occupied and concerned with that which belongs to us as a battle for GROWTH & DEVELOPMENT in the interest of cultivating our minds, speech, manners, character, conduct and skills through training study, instruction and examples. Learning the systems of financial management ranging from family budgets to owning and operating small businesses to stocks, bonds and understanding the national budget; becoming aware of and involved with the political processes of our community, City, State and Nation so that we may become active participants in making those governmental decisions, laws and policies that affect our daily lives, as well as changing our attitude and conduct toward society that we may become more socially compatible and expand our circle of acquaintances to include the middle and upper classes of society by prevailing upon them through intellect, business and politics as we unfold our new direction.

We believe that we are a special group of people with integrity and dignity:

ALL, as in ONE, we depend on, trust and have faith in the fact of ALL, as in ONE, existing as a unique and different family characterized by individuals made up of honesty, wholeness and righteousness of mind as well as self respect and worthiness.

We believe in The Vision of our great leader and through his vision:

ALL, as in ONE, we depend on, trust and have faith in and are surrounded by the understanding of where we have been, where we are and where we must advance if we are to survive, as revealed by he who belongs to us as a noble and dignified guide, moderator and Master of THE VISION.

We can become a reckoning power of people beyond boundaries, without measures:

ALL, as in ONE, has the ability to GROW & DEVELOP into ONE that has to be considered as being courageously strong and associated with an organized and unified group that surpasses all limitations and cannot be contained...

Continue The Struggle!!!
Rod Emery
3/10/96

ACKNOWLEDGEMENTS

GATOR: I appreciate **Dr. Cornel West** for staying true to his core values and steadfast beliefs. I respect his principles and his authentic pursuit for social justice and all righteous endeavors. I am grateful for his friendship and treasure the words he has written on my behalf. By his words and example, I know what it means to be an honorable top soldier in the struggle.

I want to thank God for **Dr. SaFiya**, the co-author of this biography, for coming into my life when she did. At the time she was a student running down the hallway of Howard University. I knew then she was the one meant to assist me with this project. You are a good friend, a great woman and a helluva co-author. A lot has happened during and at the conclusion of this book. Despite life's trials and demands or maybe because of them we have finally reached the summit, *Growth & Development for the Millennial Generation*! And the struggle continues…

To God be the glory.

Special Acknowledgement to:

David L. Spearman (cover photography) and **Charles Lowder** (graphic design).

Growth and Development for the Millennial Generation

DR. SAFIYA/ DR. SA ACKNOWLEDGEMENTS:

I appreciate you **Gator** for your wisdom, spirituality and determination. Your stealth observations, keen intuition and organic knowledge are astounding on so many levels. Thank you for being a friend.

Dr. West your intellectualism is ethereal and your fervor for life and the pursuit of righteousness is contagious. It has been a privilege and a dream come true to work with you and fellowship in your esteemed company.

For your respective contributions to this effort
I would like to thank:
**Corey Anderson, L. Kahlil Gross,
Dr. Leone Lettsome, Dr. Derek Henson,
The Iweanoges,
Penelope Chaman, Montrice Lowery,
Queen Aishah & Brehima Traore,
Wendy Fullman-Taylor, Traci Leaphart,
Nubia Henderson, McPhail Martin Simon Jr.,
Kevan Ware, Chris Muhammad, Jan Jameson,
Leonardo Colemon and Paul '8' Chinnery.**

AFTERWORD

It was a warm afternoon in the fall of 1998 and I was sitting at a desk in the front of Dr. Clint Wilson's journalism class on the second floor of Howard University's School of Communications. From my peripheral I saw a man scurrying through the corridor who looked familiar. Within seconds I realized, 'I know him!' I sprang from where I was seated and rushed out into the hallway yelling, "Gator!" It is always a joy to see fellow Chicagoans so far away from home. He turned in an instant and I began, "David Hoskins is my dad and you know my mother too, Penny Jones," Gator laughed, "Yeeeah, Lil' Sheba" and then smiled, "Dave, yeah that's my man, Funny Money." He had called them both by adolescent nicknames which I knew of very well from my parent's childhood friends in Morgan Park. Although Gator was breaking track records before I yelled his name he had paused to converse with me in an attentive and unhurried manner. I recounted how I had watched his aldermanic run together with my parents, our fingers crossed for his success. I learned that Gator was in town for Congressional Black Caucus and at Howard for a meeting with actor/ producer Bill Duke, then Chair of the Radio/TV/Film Department. We were both planning to attend a CBC soiree that evening hosted by one of Chicago's Congressmen, Bobby L. Rush (D-Illinois, 1st

District), for whom I was working as an intern on Capitol Hill. We exchanged information and vowed someday to work on a project.

Eight years passed before we again crossed paths, this time the meeting was a somber occasion. I was standing at the head of a long table in the basement of Mt. Calvary Baptist Church on Chicago's Southside to greet a never-ending line of repast guests who had gathered earlier to celebrate the life and memory of my father. I was pleasantly surprised and genuinely touched when Gator approached from the line of guests to pay his respects. After an extended conversation which included the discussion of my recently self-published manuscript, marriage and the attainment of a master's degree we promised that we would collaborate on a book.

Across the miles and over a period of six years, we worked on our book project which evolved through several phases and survived countless hiatuses. Between DC (sometimes New York) and Chicago we engaged in a series of candid discussions and deliberate interviews until finally we produced a book that is conversant in tone. Altogether it preserves the voice of our protagonist while offering the reader academic insight into the topics being addressed.

In 2012, we had attained our goal of generating a

completed manuscript and a foreword written by the esteemed Dr. Cornel West. In 1994, when I first read *Race Matters* my soul was stirred and I determined to someday hear Dr. West speak in person. By 2004, Dr. West had become a significant part of my development as an academician and humanitarian when suddenly my intellect was further roused by the astuteness articulated in *Democracy Matters*. As a doctoral student at Jackson State University, I often cited Dr. West and vociferously resolved that one day I would have the privilege of meeting and working with him in some capacity. I can scratch that off my 'Bucket List' now. Thank you again Dr. West and many thanks to you my dear brother-uncle-friend, Gator.

So, merrily we had set out with our completed manuscript, all about the business of being printed- having already secured a 'deal' from a major publisher. We endured lengthy political meandering leading to a retracted publishing agreement and a brief interlude with lethargic editors at another publishing house. Subsequently, we resolved that *Murder to Excellence* was much too time sensitive and critical to the social and political growth and development of the millennial generation to stagnate in a literary abyss while publishing elites determined whose voices were noteworthy to be heard.

Thus, one year from its completion and 15 years from our initial pledge, I established Ubiquitous Press and we set out to self-publish, *Murder to Excellence: Growth and Development for the Millennial Generation, The Autobiography of Wallace 'Gator' Bradley, Urban Translator.*

Dr. SaFiya
SaFiya D. Hoskins, Ph.D.
Washington, DC
December 2013

ONWARD: TO STATEVILLE

I thank GOD that Reverend Al Sharpton let it be known publicly at the historic NAN Town Hall Meeting in Chicago on December 19, 2013 that he would love to go behind the walls of Stateville to do his National Radio Talk Show *Keeping It Real* as long as the Governor, the Warden and we (United In Peace, Inc.) "Make sure that after the show he can leave." I thank GOD that he allowed the Governor to hear the people and stay true to his word when he said everybody has to do what they can to turn the tide against Senseless Shootings and Killings of African Americans by other African-Americans in particular and Americans by other Americans in general; and, for having Ms. Gladyse Taylor Assistant Director of the Illinois Department of Corrections at the Town Hall Meeting.

Since the 1990s, I've had a working relationship with Rev. Al Sharpton. He was the one who asked Rev. Jesse L. Jackson to include me in the January 24, 1994 delegation (lead by Rev. Jackson) to visit President Bill Clinton at the White House in the Oval Office; and, with S.A. Godinez, Director of Illinois Department of Corrections from 1991-1995 when he was the Warden of Statesville. During that period, I was permitted, along with business/ spiritual/ community leaders; elected and appointed officials; and, anti-gang violence activist to go behind the walls and meet with the inmates so that we could work together UNITED

IN PEACE to turn the tide against Senseless Shootings and Killings, and it worked.

I will include Geri Patterson, Toure Muhammad and Mark Allen on United In Peace, Inc.'s list. The Rev and I have let it be known to the public what he wants to do and is willing to do and when he can do it. Governor Quinn has let it be known that we all have to do what we can in order to turn the tide against Senseless Shootings and Killings of African-Americans by other African-Americans in particular and all Americans in general by having Ms. Taylor attend the Town Hall Meeting to witness for herself Reverend Al Sharpton's commitment, focus and purpose.

I told Moe that she and Bland need to get the NAN list together to include, Floyd, Rev. Hatch, Rev. Acree and whoever Rev. Al wants to be on the list- and it needs to be in place by Monday evening, December 23rd. This isn't my opinion; this is what's required per IDOC and Warden Lemke's request. Once NAN has the list together on professional letterhead I will get it to the proper personnel.

Organization of this delegation to Stateville Prison is a conceptual effort of United In Peace, Inc., NAN, IDOC, the inmates behind the walls of Stateville; and, Governor Quinn and his administration to continue to work United In Peace to turn the tide against Senseless Shootings and Killings of African-Americans by other African Americans.

The Autobiography of Wallace Gator Bradley, Urban Translator

Wallace 'Gator' Bradley
Chicago, IL
December 2013

PHOTOGRAPHS

The Autobiography of Wallace Gator Bradley, Urban Translator

Gator's march to be wedded to Terri in Israel

3 Brothers in the Kaifar (Israel), Bro. Cohane Ohmahn, Ank Gabone and Gator (Kahdmiel)

Growth and Development for the Millennial Generation

Wallace Gator Bradley, Bun B, Congresswoman Maxine Waters, J. Prince of Rap-A-Lot Records, Anzel (Red Boy) Jennings and Urban Translator Sincere Al-Amin at CBC 2013 in Washington, D C

Rev. Al Sharpton, Rev. Ira Acree, Rev. Marshall Hatch, Ms. Gladyse Taylor, Wallace Gator Bradley

The Autobiography of Wallace Gator Bradley, Urban Translator

Rev. Al Sharpton and Wallace Gator Bradley

Growth and Development for the Millennial Generation

Dr. Michael Eric Dyson and Wallace Gator Bradley
at CBC 2013 in Washington, D C

Co-authors discussing book business at CBC 2013 in Washington, DC

Mother Mrs. Ida

First cousins Jimmy and Jerry Rooks (twins), brother James Kelly (Mr. Rooks), sister Patricia Bradley (wearing the hat) and Diane Kyle.

From Gangster Disciple -to- Growth and Development
Wallace "Gator" Bradley, Rev. Jesse L. Jackson Sr. and President Bill Clinton

Wallace Gator Bradley and Larry Hoover
after his meeting with President Bill Clinton

The Autobiography of Wallace Gator Bradley, Urban Translator

Wallace Gator Bradley during his aldermanic run

Wallace Gator Bradley and Larry Hoover holding Kahdmiel

Growth and Development for the Millennial Generation

Gator in prayer at the 1993 Gang Peace Summit in Cleveland, OH

Son Leviticus at Dunham private school in Baton Rouge, LA.
Graduated Valedictorian

Daughter Afrika Bradley, grandaughter Porsche Bradley, grandson Dewayne

Great Grandson Mekhi at the White Sox baseball game.

Growth and Development for the Millennial Generation

Son Thomas Watson

Son Waitari at Tulane University. He graduated from Tulane.

Proud father at son Kahdmiel Malik Bradley's high school graduation.

Growth and Development for the Millennial Generation

Kahdmeil and his mom Terri Marsh-Bradley proving they voted.

Son Kahdmeil, a new registered voter.

The Autobiography of Wallace Gator Bradley, Urban Translator

Daughter Afrika proving she voted.

Son Kahdmeil's first day at Easstern Illinois University.

Growth and Development for the Millennial Generation

Larry Hoover Jr. and Wallace Gator Bradley
at BSO Weekend 10-Year Anniversary

The Autobiography of Wallace Gator Bradley, Urban Translator

Chicago Mayor Rahm Emanuel, Congresswoman Maxine Waters from California, University of Chicago President Dr. Wayne Watson

Cook County Commissioner Jerry Iceman Butler and Wallace Gator Bradley

Growth and Development for the Millennial Generation

JERRY BUTLER
COUNTY COMMISSIONER

OFFICE OF THE
BOARD OF COMMISSIONERS OF COOK COUNTY
118 NORTH CLARK STREET
CHICAGO, ILLINOIS 60602
312 603-6391
312 603-5671 FAX

It is a typical cold January morning in Chicago, wind chill between 30 and 40 degrees below zero

I am standing on the corner bus stop asking people on their way to work at six o'clock in the morning to sign my petition for candidate at large to the Cook County Board of Commissioners. A few feet from me is a brother hunched down in his overcoat, hat slanted to the side looking just a little bit shady shouting to passersby and commuters "Come meet the Iceman, Jerry Butler he is running for Cook County Commissioner". Some people stop to say hello and sign the petition. Most ignore him and me; others say nothing, shake their heads no and keep walking as if we aren't even there, talk about a cold shoulder!

As I wait to say thank you for those who signed the petition list I wondered why is he here? Sure, I am hip as is he to the "Quid pro Quo". "Something for something" but this man is broke betting on the come. I am thinking there probably won't be any Quo for this Quid. His name is Wallace Gator Bradley and this book is his story.

Jerry Iceman Butler
Cook County Commissioner

Gator outside of City Hall in Chicago

Father Michael Pfieger and Wallace Gator Bradley
at New Mt. Pilgram M.B.C.

Growth and Development for the Millennial Generation

Wallace Gator Bradley and Congressman Danny Davis from Chicago, Il.

Gator in action with Congressmen Bobby L. Rush and Danny K. Davis

The Autobiography of Wallace Gator Bradley, Urban Translator

Orlando Lando Magic Henry and Wallace Gator Bradley
BOS 10-Year Anniversary

Wallace Gator Bradley with Urban Translator protege Orlando Lando
Magic Henry at Kelly Ingraham Park in Birmingham, AL

Growth and Development for the Millennial Generation

Wallace Gator Bradley expressing himself.

Brother in Growth and Development
Ghetto Prisoner Clothing in Minnesota

The Autobiography of Wallace Gator Bradley, Urban Translator

Waka Flocka and sons on the Southside of Chicago.

Lupe Fiasco

Growth and Development for the Millennial Generation

Noble Ameer Ali, Executive Director
and Acting Chairman of United in Peace, Inc. and Wallace Gator Bradley

Tavis Smiley, Wallace Gator Bradley and Dr. Cornel West
at Chicago book signing for the Rich and the Rest of Us.

Dr. SaFiya D. Hoskins, (then a Howard University undergraduate) and Wallace Gator Bradley at CBC in 1998

Co-authors Dr. SaFiya D. Hoskins, and Wallace Gator Bradley in 2011

Growth and Development for the Millennial Generation

Co-authors Dr. SaFiya D. Hoskins
and Wallace Gator Bradley dropping science

Co-authors Dr. SaFiya D. Hoskins
and Wallace Gator Bradley handling business

The Autobiography of Wallace Gator Bradley, Urban Translator

Dr. SaFiya D. Hoskins, Wallace Gator Bradley and Dr. Cornel West

Dr. SaFiya Hoskins, Gator and Dr. West in dialogue

Growth and Development for the Millennial Generation

Rev. Jesse Jackson, Sr; Mellody Hobson and George Lucas

Former New York Mayor
David Dinkins

Kedar Massenberg

The Autobiography of Wallace Gator Bradley, Urban Translator

The Roosevelt Hotel in Manhattan

Growth and Development for the Millennial Generation

Times Square

"Rev. Al" Book Signing on Fifth Avenue in Manhattan

"Rev. Al"

The Autobiography of Wallace Gator Bradley, Urban Translator

"Growth & Development"

Dr. SaFiya D. Hoskins
and Wallace 'Gator' Bradley
"Growth &
Development"

The Autobiography of Wallace Gator Bradley, Urban Translator

www.unitedinpeaceinc.org

www.drsafiyahoskins.com

www.ingramcontent.com/pod-product-compliance
Lightning Source LLC
Chambersburg PA
CBHW051748040426
42446CB00007B/265